The RODGERS and HART Song Book

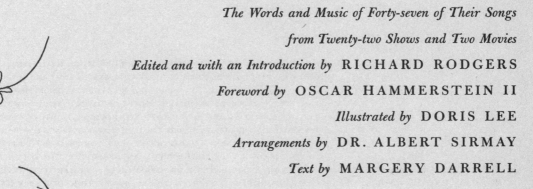

The Words and Music of Forty-seven of Their Songs

from Twenty-two Shows and Two Movies

Edited and with an Introduction by RICHARD RODGERS

Foreword by OSCAR HAMMERSTEIN II

Illustrated by DORIS LEE

Arrangements by DR. ALBERT SIRMAY

Text by MARGERY DARRELL

A Fireside Book
Published by Simon and Schuster

IF YOU WANT TO USE THIS BOOK ON A PIANO AND WOULD LIKE TO HAVE IT
OPEN AT ANY PAGE AND LIE FLAT ON THE MUSIC RACK —

LAY IT ON A FLAT SURFACE.
OPEN IT TO THE FIRST PAGE.
RUN THE TIP OF YOUR FINGER (NOT YOUR FINGERNAIL) FROM THE TOP OF THE PAGE TO
THE BOTTOM PRESSING DOWN HARD AS CLOSE AS POSSIBLE TO THE SPINE OF THE BOOK.
REPEAT THIS FOR EACH PAGE IN THE BOOK.

Table of Contents

V

Foreword

BY Oscar Hammerstein II

I MET LARRY FIRST. We were both actors in a Columbia Varsity Show. He had written a burlesque of the silent movies which had been very loosely interpolated into the story of the play. I don't remember much about this except that Larry played Mary Pickford. This would, of course, be unforgettable. The blonde curly wig didn't go very well with his thick black eyebrows, but it was not meant to. There was nothing subtle about varsity show satire in those days (circa 1915). Imitating the way movie ingénues were chased around trees by playful but purehearted heroes, Larry skipped and bounced around the stage like an electrified gnome. I think of him always as skipping and bouncing. In all the time I knew him, I never saw him walk slowly. I never saw his face in repose. I never heard him chuckle quietly. He laughed loudly and easily at other people's jokes and at his own too. His large eyes danced, and his head would wag. He was alert and dynamic and fun to be with.

After the Saturday matinee of this same Varsity Show, while the ballroom of the Hotel Astor was being cleared for the dancing that followed all performances, a fraternity brother, Morty Rodgers came up to me. He had in tow a boy about twelve years old, a smaller and darker version of himself, his kid brother, Dick. As we were being introduced I noted, with satisfaction, young Richard's respectful awe in the presence of a college junior whom he had just seen playing one of the chief parts in the Varsity Show. I, too, was conscious of my current glory and, realizing what a treat it must be for the child to meet me, I was my most gracious and courteous self—a man about nineteen trying to be a man about town. Whenever I made this effort I always finished far south of Beau Brummell and much nearer Ichabod Crane.

I saw Dick a few more times that year. Morty brought him up to the fraternity house and I heard him play on our bruised and beaten piano. We all liked him—a cute kid. In my memory of him, during this period, he wore short pants. He tells me now that by that time he had already put on long pants. All right, but in my memory he wore short pants. This impression—or illusion—is never quite absent from my current conception of him. Behind the sometimes too serious face of an extraordinarily talented composer and a sensationally successful theatrical producer, I see a dark-eyed little boy in short pants. The frequent overlapping of these two pictures is an element in what I consider to be my sound understanding of Dick and my affection for him.

It is not just my middle-aged weakness for reminiscence that led me to begin my appraisal of Rodgers and Hart by describing them when they were very young. The essence of the work they did together was its youth. They stayed young and adventurous and never lost an attractive impudence that was very much their own. At the outset, lacking a proper reverence for their elders and predecessors, they scorned to imitate Viennese operettas or the products of the local masters—Victor Herbert and Henry Blossom; Bolton, Wodehouse, and Kern; Harbach and Friml. They started something else, a kind of entertainment that soon became known as a "Rodgers and Hart Show." It had an amateur quality—amateur in the sense that its creators seemed to have had fun doing the job. In their extraordinary development as theatrical craftsmen, they never lost this gift for retaining their early character—a couple of lively New York kids, products of their town and their time.

A year or so after I had left law school I was on a Columbia University Players Club committee, appointed to choose the Varsity Show for that year. The script submitted by Dick and Larry won the competition quite easily. From time to time, after that, they would come up to my house and play songs they had written. One of these was "Manhattan." They wrote it several years before it landed on Broadway in the

Garrick Gaieties. And how it landed! How swift was the welcome, how wide-open were the arms of the town for the newness and brightness of this sassy little revue!

In addition to "Manhattan," the *Garrick Gaieties* had several other songs I knew. I liked them for their original rhymes and gay tunes, but I hadn't the perception or the courage to predict their professional success. They were, in my opinion, too literate, too complicated to become popular. I wished that the public would accept songs of this quality, but I was quite sure they wouldn't. Now here's the obvious question: if I liked them so much why didn't I assume that a great many other people were as bright and discriminating as I? It was because I hadn't yet learned that I was part of the world, going along with it, improving my taste as others improved theirs. I was pretty young myself, and inexperienced, and trying to get started in the theatre. I might, therefore, be forgiven for underrating the intelligence of the public and placing it far below my own. But I would not forgive myself for making this mistake today. And I do not forgive the hundreds of theatre, picture, radio, and television producers who continue to serve up products deemed "commercial" instead of works which they intensely and sincerely admire. The quick rise of Rodgers and Hart is a perfect illustration of how eagerly the public runs to meet something new and good, surfeited as they are with stale and imitative professionalism.

Climbing down from my soapbox, I will proceed to the business of discussing the music of my friend, Richard Rodgers. Music is a difficult subject—anybody's music. Words are easier to analyze. Everyone speaks and writes words. Few can write music. Its creation is a mystery. There are mathematical principles to guide its construction, but no mere knowledge of these can produce the emotional eloquence some music attains. We are made sad or happy, romantic, thoughtful, disturbed or peaceful by someone else's singing heart. To me this is a most exciting and inexplicable phenomenon. I should hate to be a music critic with the task of telling people what is good or bad in a musical composition or what are its component elements. One might as well try to explain to a group of children at the seaside the chemistry of salt water and sand, and the source of the sunlight or the breeze that romps with them along the shore. Certain experiences have an effect on us quite beyond the capacity of any symbols that can be written on paper, and what music can sometimes do to us is quite beyond the ken and lingo of academicians.

I am not a trained musician. As a librettist I use music as a tool that a kind composer has given me, but I have no idea where he got it. I do have some idea of how music can affect an audience in a theatre, and only within this limited area do I consider myself qualified to discuss the work of Richard Rodgers. He is essentially a composer for plays. He writes music to depict story and character and is, therefore, himself a dramatist. He is not an abstractionist in any sense and, as far as I can see, he has no interest in the mere creation of sound, however unusual or ingenious. He composes in order to make words fly higher or cut deeper than they would without the aid of his music.

He has written songs with only two men, Lorenz Hart and me. This is unusual. In the history of light music, I know of only three instances where an author and composer were permanently and exclusively linked: Gilbert and Sullivan, Rodgers and Hart, and Rodgers and Hammerstein. Before my collaboration with Dick, I wrote with Jerome Kern, Sigmund Romberg, Rudolf Friml, Vincent Youmans, Herbert Stothart, and at least a dozen other collaborators. This promiscuity is more typical of our craft. It is interesting that of the three instances of collaborative fidelity, Rodgers is in two of them. This is significant, I think, because it illustrates a sense of pattern and constructive purpose which never leaves him. This is not just professional habit, but a view of life. He is impatient with people who believe in good luck and bad luck, and he rejects mysticism as an explanation for anything. (In his heart he is

far more a mystic than he knows he is. This is my belief, but he would never agree, and we shall never have time to argue it out with each other. We shall always be too busy delineating characters in our plays to spend very much time on ourselves. A good thing, too.)

To write with one collaborator after another, to turn out a series of disconnected theatrical projects, would be unattractive to Dick. He is essentially a planner and a builder. These qualities come out clearly in his music. His melodies are clean and well-defined. His scores are carefully built, logically allied to the stories and characters they describe. No overgrown forests or weed-clogged meadows of music here, but neat rows of tenderly grown flowers on well-kept lawns. Pseudo-artists and dilettante critics might interpret these comments as disparaging. The impulsive creator of "overgrown forests" of music might seem a more powerful and more important and more rugged fellow. Speaking for myself, I am bored with undisciplined talent. The intertwining vines and aimless vegetation that spring from careless genius are of little use to a world which suffers from obscurity, and not from too much clarity. Life is so short that no musician has the right to expect any appreciable number of people to devote any appreciable part of their listening lives to the wild free notes that dribble from his talented but casual fingers. A large number of musical compositions, a large number of grand operas and light operas, are too long, too carelessly put together, and fail for this reason. They are not above the heads of the public. They are just not worthy of the public because the creative artist involved has been too self-indulgent actually to finish off his job.

In his chosen field of light dramatic music, Rodgers' work is never tentative or indefinite. Each melody adheres to the purpose for which it was put into a play. It is romantic, funny, or sad according to the situation for which it was written and the character required to sing it. Most of the songs in this volume are gay and bright and brisk in spirit. Even the music of the love ballads is, for the most part, lighthearted because the lyrics were written in that vein. The stories of the plays for which these songs were written were light stories. It is no accident that the best words I can find to describe these songs are the very words I used in my first paragraph, describing Larry Hart. I said that he was always "skipping and bouncing," and that he was "alert and dynamic and fun to be with." Larry's humor and spryness are matched perfectly by Dick's melodic resourcefulness and the persistent, pulsating beat he puts beneath every tune. He has a way of making a melody appear to be going faster than it is really being played. When a song is actually played at a very fast tempo, the singer is handicapped in projecting the lyric and the listener is handicapped because of the singer's embarrassment. With Dick's appreciation of lyric values he would never permit a song to be played too fast or too loud, yet you think of these songs as fast songs: "Sentimental Me," "Manhattan," "The Girl Friend," "Where's That Rainbow?," "You Took Advantage of Me." Play these in a fairly slow, four-four time. Sing them in that time and yet observe how quickly they seem to be moving. I think it is because of that "pulsating beat," a sustained sharpness of accent in the bass.

Even the love ballads, which perforce must be slower and sung with more sentiment, even these seem to have a pace beyond the speed at which they are actually played and sung. "Here in My Arms," "My Heart Stood Still," "Where or When," "With a Song in My Heart"—these have strong melodic lines, and one line moves on to another without any long pauses between. Composer and lyricist get on with what they have to say, say it clearly and effectively and

without interruption, without getting gooey in their sentiment, without becoming ponderous.

In the second decade of their collaboration Rodgers and Hart began to take waltzes more seriously. They had started writing at a time when American composers were dodging theme songs in three-quarter time. Waltzes had been the stock in trade of the Viennese school. Victor Herbert was an American exponent of the Viennese school as were Romberg and Friml. But Jerome Kern, Lou Hirsch, George Gershwin, Vincent Youmans, and Richard Rodgers seceded from these traditions and one of the results of their secession was to reduce the waltz to a minor position in their scores. Every once in a while, however, the natural charm of this tempo would assert itself, and these rebels would write fine waltzes, in spite of their alleged prejudice. "The Most Beautiful Girl in the World," "Falling in Love with Love," and "Lover" are three of the strongest songs in this Rodgers and Hart collection. They have become standard American waltzes played year after year, all over the world. One of my favorites is "Wait Till You See Her," a song that was placed in their last show, *By Jupiter*, but eventually cut from the score. Read it and play it and sing it and see if you don't agree with me that it should be revived some day to take its proper place in their impressive catalogue of waltzes.

Any contemporary, looking through the pages of this book, must feel grateful to Rodgers and Hart for all the joy they have given us. This is a group of lovable songs. It is not alone the writers who can be proud of them. We can all be proud that they were written in our country and in our time.

OSCAR HAMMERSTEIN II

The RODGERS *and* HART *Song Book*

Introduction

BY RICHARD RODGERS

IN REGARD *to Larry Hart's words I am perhaps the greatest living expert. Larry and I worked together for over twenty-four years, from the time I was sixteen and he was twenty-three until his death in 1943 when I was forty and he forty-seven. This was possibly the oldest partnership in the history of the theatre, with the exception of the Shuberts who have been united by blood as well as predilection. I have no fear that my devotion to these lyrics is solely emotional. It was necessary, during all those years, to examine these words and work with them not only in the stage of composition but in the stage of projection (the process of getting actors to sing the words intelligibly and to see that no distractions in the way of bad lighting or loud orchestra interfered). Mr. Hart's composer would have to be highly aware of the phonetic subtleties and semantic overtones in these lyrics, and I believe I have always been very much alive to them.*

In a larger sense there is something I should like this book to be. I think Mr. Hart deserves a memorial. It is true that his songs are sung many thousands of times a day, in theatres, on records, on radios, and on people's tongues, but this book will put them in people's hands.

Larry had only one pride that I was ever able to discover. That was his work. He didn't care about the way he looked or where he lived. He wasn't concerned with the social or financial status of his friends or what row he sat in at an opening. He did care tremendously, however, about the turn of a phrase and the mathematical exactness of an interior rhyme. This book has many such phrases and rhymes, and so I think it would have pleased him as it pleases me.

1

Before Hart, only P. G. Wodehouse had made any real assault on the intelligence of the song-listening public and even his attempts were comparatively tentative and not particularly courageous. Larry, right from the beginning, took the bull by the horns and threw it over the proscenium arch. His lyrics knew, for instance, that love was not especially devised for boy and girl idiots of fourteen and he expressed himself to that extent.

In 1925 he was able to proclaim right out in public, and no one objected, that the "Freudian" subconscious motivated a great deal of our acting and thinking. For a song writer this would be considered radical even today, but Mr. Hart didn't scare easily. By way of proof there is a song (not included in this collection) we wrote in 1920 called "You Can't Fool Your Dreams." This was a great many years before any of us had heard of psychoanalysis, and I mention it here, not to show that our thinking was particularly advanced, but to demonstrate our willingness to employ subject matter hitherto ignored by the songwriting profession. This desire to explore did not stop with the individual songs. It extended to the shows themselves. Looking at the table of contents of this book, it is clear that there must have been an almost continual search for diversification of subject matter. These range from a little revue through romantic fantasy and a musical circus, to political satire.

The reader may be curious about the work methods we employed in writing these songs and shows. Our work habits were almost as diversified as the subject matter. We always had a distaste for artistic self-pampering, as I still have today, and only rarely did we ever take one of those hide-out trips so popular with writers. It was when we were preparing On Your Toes *for rehearsals. Our writing had been interrupted by extracurricular pressures so often that we took a suite at the Ritz in Atlantic City for a week end in the hope that we could finish one of three important songs that remained to be done. We returned to New York on Monday with all three completed, and I remember that we felt happy and rested.*

Only one thing remained constant in Larry's approach to his job.

2

He hated doing it and loved it when it was done. There was the never-ceasing routine of trying to find him, locking him up in a room, and hoping to fire his imagination so that actual words would get down on paper. It wasn't wise to leave him alone for a moment because he would simply disappear and have to be found all over again. His pencil would fly over the paper and soon the most difficult part of all would begin: the material had to be edited and he loathed changing any word once it was written down. When the immovable object of his unwillingness to change came up against the irresistible force of my own drive for perfection, the noise could be heard all over the city. Our fights over words were furious, blasphemous, and frequent, but even in their hottest moments we both knew that we were arguing academically and not personally. I think I am quite safe in saying that Larry and I never had a single personal argument with each other.

Larry and I were brought together in 1918 by a mutual friend who knew that each of us needed a collaborator. It shocks me to realize that this happened thirty-three years ago, but it excites me to think of the technical content of the discussion that went on that Sunday afternoon. I heard for the first time from the master (he was twenty-three, and seven years my senior) of interior rhymes, feminine rhymes, triple rhymes, and false rhymes. I listened with astonishment as he launched a diatribe against song writers who had small intellectual equipment and less courage, the boys who failed to take advantage of every opportunity to inch a little further into territory hitherto unexplored in lyric writing. "If you wanted to write about New York, you didn't have to be as naïve as 'East Side—West Side.' " A couple of years later he said,

> "We'll have Manhattan
> The Bronx and Staten
> Island, too."

and Rodgers and Hart had written their first hit, although we weren't to find it out for several years.

Heywood Broun in reviewing our first show, Poor Little Ritz Girl, *in 1920 said that it was obvious that the lyric writer "had his ear to the ground and not to the nearest stage door." He might have said that again in 1943 had he been able to review the revival of* Connecticut Yankee. *If the reader will examine the words of "To Keep My Love Alive," written nearly twenty-five years after Heywood Broun's review, he will find the same inability on Larry's part to succumb to a cliché or to rhyme any way but brilliantly.*

It seems to me that Larry's later lyrics were of a higher degree of excellence than his early ones and that they achieved this through a growing maturity of their own. Later on he seemed almost to substitute warmth for wit, and while he really didn't know how not to be clever, he began to show off less and to be more concerned with emotion. "Where or When," for instance, had much of the philosophical in it, and I can think of no lyric more touched with tenderness than "Funny Valentine." In the face of the pin-wheel brilliance of some of Larry's work, one is inclined to forget the deeper phases of his writing.

Larry and I met artistically like two volatile chemicals in a retort, and the explosion resulted in a series of songs, nearly all of which are now forgotten. This same mutual friend who had introduced us felt that we should meet Lew Fields—what our friend had in mind here was that this team of young writers should form a contact with a successful producer. At that time, Lew Fields had a musical show called A Lonely Romeo *playing at the Casino Theatre. One Sunday afternoon at his home in Far Rockaway I played at least a dozen of these songs for Mr. Fields. (One of his sons was present at the time. This was Herbert, who subsequently wrote the book for many of our musical shows.) Mr. Fields liked particularly a song called "Any Old Place with You" and a few weeks later interpolated it in the score of* A Lonely Romeo. *It was sung by Eve Lynn and Alan Hale. I suppose it will seem pretty sophomoric, but perhaps this can be excused on the grounds that I wasn't to be a sophomore for another three years. As it was the first song Larry and I had done professionally, perhaps it deserves a place at the beginning of the collection.*

RICHARD RODGERS

Any Old Place with You

Brightly

mf

mp

There is a rail-road a-round lov-er's lane
We'll mad-ly fly o-ver hill and down dale

And the con-duc-tor is you._____
In lit-tle Cu-pid's ex-press._____

My heart goes fast-er than an-y old train,
I'm at the throt-tle and I'll nev-er fail,

Trav - el with me please do. ____
Till life's long road is done. ____

Refrain (in strict 4/4)

We'll melt in Syr - i - a, freeze in Si - be - ri - a,
From old Vir - gin - i - a, or Ab - ys - sin - i - a,

Neg - li - gee in Tim - buk - tu, ____
We'll go straight to Hal - i - fax, ____

In dream - y Por - tu - gal
I've got a ma - ni - a

I'm goin' to court you gal, an - cient Rome we'll paint a - new.
for Penn - syl - va - ni - a, e - ven ride in Lon - don hacks.

Life would be cheer-i-er on Lake Su-pe-ri-or,
I'll call each dude a pest, you like in Bu-da-pest,

How would Pe-kin do?_____ I'm goin' to cor-ner ya
Oh for far Pe-ru!_____ I'll go to hell for ya

in Cal-i-for-ni-a, An-y old place___ with
or Phil-a-del-phi-a, An-y old place___ with

you.
you.___

PART ONE
1925-1928

Garrick Gaieties

EVERYTHING about *Garrick Gaieties* was young, hopeful, and spontaneous. It gave the impression of having been whipped up casually in a two-room apartment by a few kids having a party—and many parties have actually cost more. It had a cast of unknowns, an eleven-piece orchestra, cutout scenery, a tight five-thousand-dollar budget, and songs by two young men in their twenties of whom the Twenties were as yet unaware.

In a season which had already seen forty-six musicals, the Theatre Guild produced the *Gaieties* with the hopeful notion that it might pay for tapestries in the new Guild theatre. A diffident, undersized advertisement ran just before the opening on May 17, 1925: "The show will be very good although the seats are very cheap . . . $2.20 in the orchestra, $1.65 and $1.10 in the balcony; two performances only (unless you insist on more) will be given on Sunday, May 17, at 2:30 and 8:30."

More, much more, was insisted on — through a June heat wave and for twenty-five additional weeks. These new young song writers, Richard Rodgers and Lorenz Hart, had stumbled on a gold mine. Or so Broadway said. But it was Broadway that had stumbled on the gold mine, and, as usual, it had taken Broadway a long time. Rodgers and Hart had been maneuvering to be stumbled on ever since 1917.

They thought hard before saying yes to contributing words and music to *Garrick Gaieties*. Both had a growing feeling that it was time they got paid for their work. Some time back Rodgers had begun borrowing five dollars from a friend every time he had a date. He now owed a hundred and five dollars and was thinking reluctantly about selling children's underwear. ("And, failing that, my own," he adds.)

Until the sudden and overwhelming success at the Garrick, they had had only the most modest kind of recognition. In 1920, a committee, of which Oscar Hammerstein II was a member, had chosen a Rodgers and Hart score for the Columbia University Varsity Show. The now defunct *Globe* had these cautious comments to make the morning after: "We do not know what Mr. Hart proposes to do with his young life — but if he wishes to have an avocation, lyric writing will give him, we think, as much as the average lawyer in, say, Ridgway, Elk County, Pennsylvania, earns." And of Mr. Rodgers, "Several of his tunes are capital. We have not heard of Mr. Rodgers before. We have a suspicion we will hear of him again."

Rodgers and Hart became Rodgers & Hart with the debut of *Garrick Gaieties*. The show had all the wit, melody, and informality that people missed in elaborate revues like the Shuberts' *Artists and Models* or the *Ziegfeld Follies*. Robert Benchley called it "the most civilized show in town." Libby Holman made a sultry debut, and you can still find batches of lapel-grabbing middlesters and oldsters around New York whose eyes will brighten and whose tongues will start wagging if you give them a chance to hold forth on the charm of June Cochrane's and Sterling Holloway's singing of the show's main hit, "Manhattan."

"Strangely enough," wrote Larry Hart, "it is a number with very intricate and elaborate rhymes, though the song hit of a show is usually a very simple one with monosyllabic words. 'Manhattan' gets several encores at every performance, is the laughing hit of the show, and also the music strain that people carry away with them."

The Guild got its new tapestries. And four of the *Garrick Gaieties* songs are the main reasons why. (Sticklers will want it pointed out that one, "Mountain Greenery," comes from the second *Garrick Gaieties*, which followed within a year.)

Dearest Enemy

IF YOU happened to open your New York *Times* to the theatrical section on the morning of September 20, 1925, if you noticed that Alexander Woollcott was reviewing the opening of a musical called *Dearest Enemy*, and if the thought crossed your mind that a musical with a historical background was a pretty radical idea, it is more than likely that your doubts were dispelled by Woollcott's reaction: "It may roughly be classified with those dramas in which the picture of the times is limited to that moment in the first act when one of the characters stops the play long enough to observe, 'Well, well, what are we coming to? Eggs went up to two cents a pound yesterday.' "

In the first act, Helen Ford made a memorable entrance. She was fished out of a river off stage and arrived clad modestly, as Woollcott recorded, "in a rather short barrel." After a few minutes of extremely pretty confusion and embarrassment, she recovered her clothes and proceeded about the real business of the show. This, in Herb Fields' charming fable of the American Revolution and a very new New York, was to fall in love with a British soldier.

The principal scene was based on the famous meal served by a loyal daughter of the Revolution, Mrs. Murray, a meal which kept the British top brass long after dinner and saved the day for General Washington. In spite of the barrel scene, which caused much talk, the show was impeccably clean. Perhaps the only moment which might be described as peccable was a demure remark made by the hostess, Mrs. Murray. When Washington sent word to detain the British, he instructed his messenger to say that he left the means entirely to her discretion. "General Washington," replied the lady, "has his vulgar moments."

But it was a song called "Here in My Arms" which drew the crowds. Would-be song writers might be interested in Larry Hart's account of his creative technique in writing it: "If I am trying to write a melodic song hit, I let Richard Rodgers get his tune first. Then I take the most distinctive melodic phrase in his tune and work on that. What I choose is not necessarily the theme or first line but the phrase which stands out. Next I try to find the meaning of that phrase and to develop a euphonic set of words to fit it. For example, in one of our songs, the first line runs like this: 'Here in my arms, it's adorable.' The distinct melodic phrase came on the word *adorable*, and the word *adorable* is the first word that occurred to me, so I used it as my pivotal musical idea. And as the melodic phrase recurs so often in the chorus, it determined my rhyme scheme. Of course, in a song of this sort the melody and the euphonics of the words themselves are really more important than the sense."

The Girl Friend

THE GIRL FRIEND made her debut in 1926, as the first of a series of fast little Rodgers & Hart musicals which were written almost yearly thereafter for production in the Vanderbilt. This show had a great deal to do with the establishment of Larry Hart as a lyricist with a superb sophistication all his own. Nothing is more typical of him than the intricate, brilliantly inevitable lines of the title song. "I saw him write a sparkling stanza to 'The Girl Friend,'" writes Rodgers, "in a hot, smelly rehearsal hall, with chorus girls pounding out jazz time and principals shouting out their lines. In half an hour he fashioned something with so many interior rhymes, so many tricky phrases and so many healthy chuckles in it that I just couldn't believe he'd written it that evening."

"The Girl Friend" has a marvelously optimistic melody which moves downward only when it has to and turns up insistently at the end. And "Blue Room," besides being one of the most popular songs ever written, is a compact object lesson in Rodgers & Hart design. The elements of this song combine perfectly to emphasize its chief characteristic — the rhythm of the melody. With only a few exceptions all the rhymes and inner rhymes occur on the same note, C. Every time you are going to hear the half note which is the center of the melody, it is preceded by the repetition of C and the rhyme. And this same half note is always the note which carries (each time higher) the word *room*, the most important word in the song. In other words, both words and music are used to underscore the note which gives the song its individuality.

Robert Benchley paid a handsome tribute to Hart when he reviewed *The Girl Friend* for *Life* (not Luce-*Life*, but the original *Life* which will be remembered partly because it had Robert Benchley as a reviewer). "Mr. Hart's lyrics," he wrote, "show unmistakable signs of the writer's having given personal thought to the matter."

Peggy-Ann

PEGGY-ANN was a study in the unusual. It violated every musical-comedy tradition, borrowed a few more from other art forms, and then violated them, too.

There was no opening chorus. In fact, for the first fifteen minutes, there was no singing or dancing at all. The plot was simply one long dream. The eternal musical-comedy love story was kidded, for once. The chorus danced in a sort of planned chaos. The lights misbehaved with a sort of wayward intelligence of their own, the spotlight was never in the right place, and the footlights and borderlights went on and off willfully.

The dancing, when it finally arrived, was an abrupt departure from the collection of speedy routines and specialty numbers which is still standard fare in musicals. Seymour Felix gave it a ballet quality and a genuine function in the show. When Peggy-Ann went from the country to her idea of New York City, the chorus made the trip with her in pantomime, changing from country to city costume on the way. The second act introduction had no dancing in it at all, and the finale (which had to be in the dark because Peggy woke up in the dark) was a slow comedy dance. Who ever heard of a musical that ended with a whisper and a laugh?

Many people did, within a few days after *Peggy-Ann* opened, even though four other shows opened the same night. By the time the critics got to it, it didn't need a kind word from anyone.

It was quite a world Peggy-Ann dreamed up. Her conception of New York, faithfully carried out on the stage, was of a place where all traffic on Fifth Avenue knocked off while the policemen went to lunch, and where society ladies munched bananas in fancy dressmakers' shops. On a yacht bearing Peggy-Ann and her loved one out to sea, the crew was suddenly seized by a morality notable among sailors, and mutinied because the lovers weren't married. And when Peggy-Ann tried to save the situation by getting married, she found herself at the ceremony in her underwear with her mother officiating, using a telephone book as a Bible. In that early day, no one seemed to bother about the darker psychiatric overtones of Peggy-Ann's dreams. The Lewis-Carroll-like whimsicality charmed all but the most prudish—and even they went home feeling that there must be something good to say about wickedness because it was so enjoyable.

Rodgers & Hart both had a particular affection for *Peggy-Ann*. Its success reaffirmed their basic view that the best way to cope with traditions in the theatre is to establish a whole new set of your own.

A Connecticut Yankee

As far back as 1921 Herb Fields and Dick Rodgers were on the right track about *A Connecticut Yankee*. They were just in the wrong year. That was when they saw the silent movie of the Mark Twain classic and decided it would make a superb musical. Rodgers immediately obtained a six-months' option on it from the Mark Twain estate. But in 1921 there was no loud demand for Rodgers and Hart, and the option died before they could do anything about it.

Six years later things were happily different. The show opened on November third, and no one who saw it ever forgot it. Billy Gaxton, playing "The Boss," got hit on the head by his girl and took a much longer count than Tunney had taken two months before. In fact, he found himself fourteen centuries in the past, in King Arthur's Camelot. By the time he woke up again in 1927, Camelot was a very unusual fifth-century town, complete with telephones, tabloids, a King Arthur who talked like President Coolidge, and billboards reading, "I would fain walk a furlong for a Camel."

It is pretty generally known that the title for "My Heart Stood Still" originated in a Paris taxicab. A carefree Parisian driver shaved another car by a fraction of an inch, instead of the usual inch-and-a-half allowed for by taxicab drivers. The girl riding in the cab turned breathlessly to Rodgers & Hart with the words, "My heart stood still," and thereby became an even more widely quoted young lady than Dorothy Parker. What isn't so well known is the fact that "My Heart Stood Still" had been written originally for a London show and had to be bought back for five thousand dollars to be put into *A Connecticut Yankee*.

There was also a little trouble about "Thou Swell." When the show opened in Philadelphia, the song left the audience cold, and after three weeks there it still hadn't grown on anybody. But Rodgers insisted that it be left in until the show opened in New York, where nobody ever thought of taking it out again. It is probably one of Larry Hart's most charming lyrics.

In 1943, after some fifteen years of constant pressure, Rodgers &

Hart sat down to bring Camelot up to date again. Principal additions were a jeep and four new songs, the main one being "To Keep My Love Alive," written for Vivienne Segal.

Present Arms

In 1926, when people were busy building Venetian lagoons in Florida and skyscrapers in Manhattan, the Mansfield Theatre went up on Forty-seventh Street, and for two years the management tried to lure people into it. Show after show opened there and closed promptly a few weeks later. But on April 30, 1928, the owners of the Mansfield went home and slept even more soundly than had their previous audiences. They had a show there called *Present Arms*.

Students of the theatre may find something vaguely familiar in the fact that *Present Arms* was a show with music by Richard Rodgers, set in the South Pacific. But it wasn't about an Army nurse who fell in love with a French planter. It concerned a buck private who fell in love with the daughter of a pineapple king.

The heroine stumbled on her Marine hero one day while he was peeling onions and was so taken with him she assumed he must be a captain. When he turned out to be a private and a plumber's son, too (the information "leaked out," as one of the characters could not restrain himself from saying), they had a fight and she stayed mad through most of the show. This made time for another romance and that reproachful favorite, "You Took Advantage of Me," which you can find in the pages to follow.

Garrick Gaieties

Moderately

We bring dra - ma to your great me - trop - o - lis, ___ We are the lit - tle thea - tre group. Each of us has built a small a - crop - o - lis ___ to hold our

one of us, Each son of us will wel-come you at the

gate.

Patter

The neigh-bor-hood Play-house may shine be - low the Mac-y - Gim-bel line,
— Pro-vince-town Play-house still owns the art of Ro-bert Ed-mond Jones,
— your at - ten-tion, man - y thanks we've brought a - long sub-scrip-tion blanks,

mp leggiero

It was built to make a ride for peo-ple on Fifth Av-e-nue. To
From the clas-sic dra - ma we're a no-ta-ble se - ces-sion-ist. We've
For the ac - tor's Thea-tre that the au - di-ence may glo-ry in. The

some-thing Os - car Wilde - ish, in a pan-to-mime or dance. Grand
mood is ver - y "Roosh - in" you can tell it at a glance. Our
things that pleased our Ma - mas such as Can-di - da's ro - mance. We

Street folk we nev - er see 'em they think the place is a mu-seum And we
bare stage may look fun - ny but it saves us lots of mon-ey And we
wear the sock and bus-kin to the taste of old John Rus-kin And we

know just what we do, Be-cause we al - ways take a chance!___
know just what we do, Be-cause we al - ways take a chance!___
know just what we do, Be-cause we nev - er take a chance!___

21

Dialogue: The Garrick Gaieties is coming down the street!
Here's where we meet our meat!

The
For

Gild - ing   the   Guild   Gild - ing   the   Guild,

We pos-sess a fine ar - tis-tic touch— Mon-ey does-n't count, not much!

Shu-berts may say, Art does - n't pay,

But we've built this co - zy lit-tle shack, Tho we lack Shu-bert's Jack!

In our cute lit-tle build-ing We're gild-ing the Guild!—

Sentimental Me

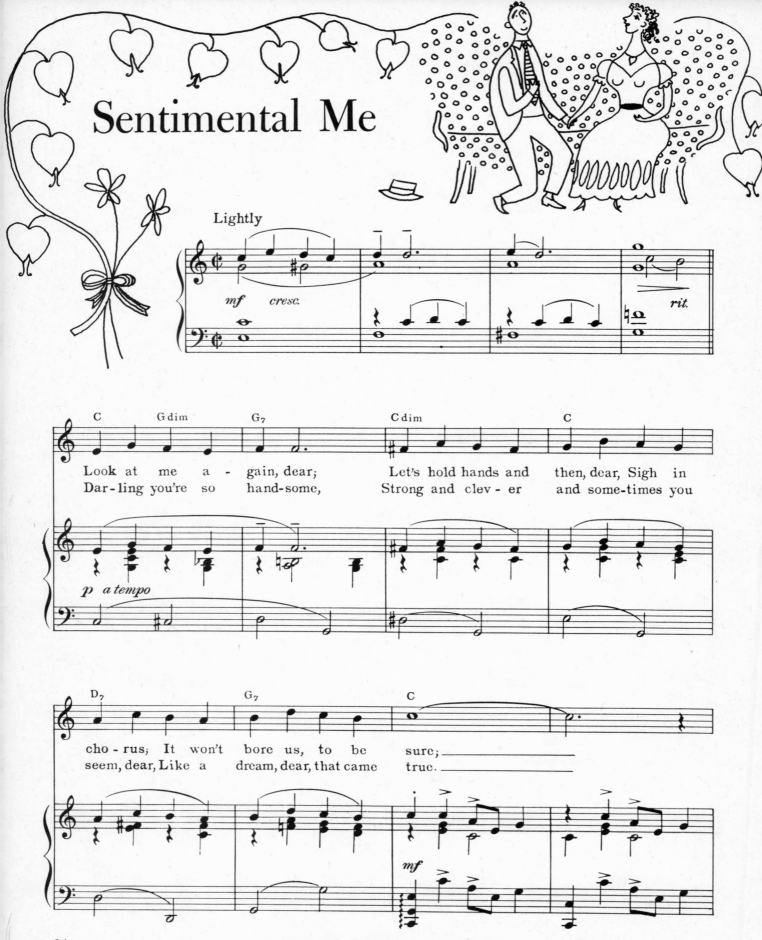

Lightly

mf *cresc.* *rit.*

p a tempo

C Gdim G7 Cdim C

Look at me a - gain, dear; Let's hold hands and then, dear, Sigh in
Dar - ling you're so hand-some, Strong and clev - er and some-times you

D7 G7 C

cho - rus; It won't bore us, to be sure; ___
seem, dear, Like a dream, dear, that came true. ___

mf

There's no mean-ing to it, Yet we o - ver - do it, With a
That's why I picked you out; Bet - ter men I threw out Of my

rel - ish that is hell - ish to en - dure;
liv - ing room while giv - ing room to you;

I am not the kind that mere - ly flirts;
I would rath - er read of love in books;

I just love and love un - til it hurts.
Love is much more pain - ful than it looks.

Refrain *(gracefully)*

Oh, sen-ti-men-tal me and poor ro-man-tic you;

Dream-ing dreams is all that we can do; We hang a - round all day and

pon-der, While both of us grow fond - er The Lord knows where we're

wan-der - ing to! I sit and sigh; you sigh and sit up -

Manhattan

Brightly

Sum-mer jour-neys to Ni - ag-'ra, And to oth- er plac- es ag-gra- vate all our

cares; We'll save our fares; I've a co - zy lit - tle flat in

what is known as old Man-hat-tan, We'll set - tle down right here in town.

From the first *Garrick Gaieties*. Copyright 1925 by Edward B. Marks Music Corporation. Copyright renewed 1952 by Richard Rodgers.

The sub - way charms us so, _____ When balm - y breez - es blow
Your bath - ing suit so thin _____ Will make the shell - fish grin
In Cen - tral Park, we'll stroll _____ Where our first kiss we stole,
Our Flat - bush flat I guess _____ Will be a great suc - cess.

To and fro; And tell me what street com - pares with Mott Street
Fin to fin; I'd like to take a sail on Ja - mai - ca
Soul to soul; Our fu - ture ba - bies we'll take to A - bie's
More or less; A short va - ca - tion On In - spir - a - tion

in Ju - ly, _____ Sweet push carts gen - tly glid - - ing
Bay with you; _____ And fair Can - ar - sie's Lake _____ we'll
I - rish Rose, _____ I hope they'll live to see _____ it
Point we'll spend _____ And in the sta - tion house _____ we'll

by;_____ The great big cit - y's a won-d'rous toy Just
view;_____ The cit - y's bus - tle can-not de - stroy The
close;_____ The cit - y's clam - or can nev - er spoil The
end_____ But Civ - ic Vir - tue can-not de - stroy The

made for a girl and boy, We'll turn Man-hat-tan In - to an isle of
dreams of a girl and boy, We'll turn Man-hat-tan In - to an isle of
dreams of a boy and goil, We'll turn Man-hat-tan In - to an isle of
dreams of a girl and boy, We'll turn Man-hat-tan In - to an isle of

joy._____
joy._____
joy._____
joy._____

Mountain Greenery

Moderately

mf

rall.

p a tempo grazioso

| C | C+ | F6 | Bb | G7 | C |

On the first of May   It is mov - ing day;
Sim - ple cook - ing means   More than French cui - sines.

| Em | Em7 | Am | F | D7 | G | G+ | C | Am6 | Adim |

Spring is here, so blow your job,   Throw your job a - way;
I've a ban - quet planned which is   sand - wich - es and beans,

| G | G+ | C | F | D7 | G7 |

Now's the time to trust   To your wan - der - lust.
Cof - fee's just as grand   With a lit - tle sand.

poco a poco cresc.

I'll search for wood, _____ So you can cook. _____ While I stand look - - ing. Beans could get no keen - er re - cep - tion in a bean - er - y. Bless our moun - tain green - er - y home. _____

Here in My Arms

Moderately and leisurely

I know a mer-ry place
I know a pret-ty place

Far from in-tru-sion. It's just the ver-y place For your se-clu-sion.
At your com-mand, sir; It's not a cit-y place, Yet near at hand, sir;

There you can while a-way Days as you clu-sion.
Here, if you loll a-way, Two hearts can hand, sir;

For me to ask my share___ Next to my heart it is
ev- er so lone-ly, I'm hold- ing on- ly air,
While here in my arms it's a- dor- a- ble!___ It's de-
plor-a- ble___ That you were nev- er there.___ there.___

41

Blue Room

Moderately

not fast

He: All my fu - ture plans, Dear, will suit your plans, Read the lit - tle
She: From all vis - i - tors And in - quis - i - tors, We'll keep our a -

blue prints;
part - ment;.

Here's your moth - er's room, Here's your
I won't change your plans, You ar -

broth - er's room, On the wall are two prints.
range your plans Just the way your heart meant;

43

Just noth-ing but kiss - es, With Mis-ter and Mis - sus On lit- tle blue chairs. { You sew your trous-seau, And { I'll wear my

Rob-in - son Cru-soe is not so far from world- ly cares As our blue room far a - way up- stairs! stairs!

The Girl Friend

Joyously

mf

rit.

He: My girl's the kind of girl for stead-y com-pa-ny. It's stead-y
She: He's ver-y short on looks but long on de-cen-cy, He's long on

p a tempo

com-pa-ny That I pre-fer._____ When
de-cen-cy, He's ver-y tame._____ But

in the Charles-ton dance I want to bump a knee, I want to
he has made an aw-ful hit with me since he, A hit with

la - dy can be. A look at this vi - sion will
la - dy can be. She ain't got no cul - ture, she's

cause a col - li - sion, She's the girl friend! _____
keen as a vul - ture, She's the girl friend! _____

She is smart, _ She's re - fined, _ How can she be
She: He is smart, _ He's re - fined, _ How can he be

real? She has heart, _ She has mind, _
real? He has heart, _ He has mind, _

Where's That Rainbow?

Moderately

very calmly

She: Trou - bles real - ly are bub - bles, they say, And I'm
He: For - tune nev - er smiles, but in my case It just

bub - bling o - ver to - day! Spring brings ros - es to
laughs right in___ my face. She: If I looked for a

peo - ple, you see, But it brings hay fe - ver to me!
horse-shoe, I spose It would bop me right in the nose.

If I have ev - er had luck, It's bad luck, that's sure. My Po - ly - an - na My luck has changed, it's stuff too, Is tough to en - dure!

My luck will var - y sure - ly, that's pure - ly a curse. got - ten From rot - ten to worse!

Refrain (*slowly with tender expression*)

Where's that rain - bow you hear a - bout?___

I know morn-ing will come, but par - don my laugh - ter!

In each sce-na - ri - o, you can de-pend on the

end, where the lov - ers a - gree. Where's that Lo-tha - ri - o,

where does he roam with his dome, vas - e - lined as can be?

It is eas-y to see al-right, __

Ev-'ry-thing's gon-na be al-right, __ Be just dan-dy for

ev-'ry-bod-y but me!

me!

poco a poco dim.

A Tree in the Park

No one else a - round, but you and me in the dark!

Just five min - utes from your door - step, I'll wait for your step to come a -

long! And the cit - y's roar be - comes a song!

While I'm wait - ing, I dis - cov - er more in your charms;

Sud-den-ly I turn a-round, and you're in my arms.

And if there's a moon a-bove you, I'll carve "I

love you," up-on the bark, Un-der-neath our lit-tle tree, in-side the

1. park!

2. park!

mf

rit.

mf

I
LOVE
YOU

59

My Heart Stood Still

He: I laughed at sweet - hearts
She: Through all my school - days

I met at schools;
I hat - ed boys;

All in - dis - creet hearts
Those Ap - ril - Fool days

Seemed ro - man - tic fools.   A house in
Brought me love - less joys.   I read my

Ice - land   Was my heart's do - main.   I
Pla - to,   Love, I thought a sin;   But

saw your eyes; Now cas - tles rise in   Spain!_____
since your kiss, I'm read - ing Mis - sus Glyn!_____

Refrain (slow but liltingly)

I took one look at you, That's all I meant to do;

That un - felt clasp of hands____ Told me so
well you knew.____ I nev - er lived at all
Un - til the thrill of that mo - ment when my heart stood
still.
still.____

Thou Swell

Calmly

In a jolly tempo

He: Babe, we are well met, As in a spell met, I lift my hel-met,
She: Thy words are queer, Sir, Un-to mine ear, Sir, Yet thou'rt a dear, Sir,

San-dy;— You're__ just dan__dy. For____ just this
to me;— Thou__ could'st woo__ me; Now____ could'st thou

here lad. You're such a fist-full, My eyes are mist-ful,
try, knight. I'd mur-mur "Swell," too, And like it well too;

Refrain (slowly, with grace)

Thou swell! Thou wit-ty! Thou sweet! Thou grand! Wouldst

kiss me pret-ty? Wouldst hold my hand? Both thine eyes are cute too;

What they do to me. Hear me hol-ler I choose a Sweet

lol-la-pa-loo-sa in thee. I'd feel so

On a Desert Island with Thee

He: Come, sit thee near; Place thy - self up-on my knee; Make an

end of thy fear, For I love but thee in Ca - me - lot.

She: Oh, no not here Where ob - served of all we'll be. Should thy

fa - ther ap - pear, He would sure - ly scold and damn a lot.

He: Care not a jot, Heark-en to my plot:

Soon we'll re - treat to a sweet spot!

Refrain (gracefully)

Oh for a year on a des - ert is - land with thee,

p a tempo

bring for thee? (We'll need   some books   to   read;)_____   *He:* Thou

needst not bring ten books a-long, If   thou wilt bring thy   looks a-long,'Twill be   e-

nough   for   me. _____   If   the heat be-gins to swel-ter,

We   won't have to fear the   sun.   We   will lie be-neath a   shel-ter

72

To Keep My Love Alive

Moderately

mf

p

I've been mar-ried and mar-ried, and of-ten I've sighed, __

I'm nev-er a brides-maid, I'm al-ways the bride; __

I __ nev-er di-vorced them, I had-n't the heart, __

Yet, re-mem-ber these sweet words, "Till death do us part."

Refrain (with care and elegance)

I mar-ried man-y men, a ton of them, and yet I was un-true to
I thought Sir George had pos-si-bil-i-ties, but his flir-ta-tions made me

none of them, be-cause I bumped off ev-'ry one of them to
ill at ease, and when I'm ill at ease, I kill at ease to

keep my love a-live. Sir Paul was frail, he looked a
keep my love a-live. Sir Charles came from a san-a-

wreck to me. At night he was a hor-se's neck to me, so
to-ri-um, and yelled for drinks in my em - po-ri-um. I

I per-formed an ap-pen-dec-to-my, to keep my love a-live! Sir
mixed one drink, he's in me-mo-ri-am, to keep my love a-live! Sir

Tho-mas had in-som-ni-a, he could-n't sleep at night, I
Fran-cis was a sing-ing bird, a night-in-gale, That's why I

bought a lit-tle ar-sen-ic, he's sleep-ing now all right. Sir
tossed him off my bal-co-ny to see if he could fly. Sir

Phil-ip played the harp, I cussed the thing. I crowned him with his harp to
Ath-el-stane in-dulged in frat-ri-cide, he killed his dad and that was

bust the thing, and now he plays where harps are just the thing, to
pat-ri-cide. One night I stabbed him by my mat-tress side, to

keep my love a - live, to keep my love a - live.
keep my love a - live, to

I keep my love a - live.

I Feel at Home with You

Moderately

He: This used to be a grump-y, crab-bed old lad;
She: I used to be a hoy-den, Boys were my hate,

Look at your beam-ish boy now.
I was a la-dy her- -mit.

This used to be a jump-y; sil - ly and sad,
I could-n't be an-noyed in mak-ing a date;

What is sim - ply joy now.
Sil - ly I would term it.

Life was a can - yon too dark to view____
You seemed so dar - ing my heart grew frail,____

Till a com - pan - ion was found like you.____
Now I like wear - ing my coat of male.____

Refrain (brightly)

I feel___ at home with you;___ You al-ways fit on___ The
I feel___ at home with you;___ Your brain___ is dumb-er___ Than

knees that___ you sit on; That's why___ I feel at home___ with
that of___ a plumb-er; That's why___ I feel at home___ with

you.___ I love___ to
you.___ I'll match___ my

roam with you.___ Each place___ that we go___ You
dome with you.___ Your brain needs___ a ton-ic___ It's

80

too.
such.

You are___ a part of me,___
You have___ no head at all,___

Some-thing___ that's giv-ing___ me rea-son___ for liv-ing;
Some-thing___ like your knob___ is used as___ a door knob;

That's why___ I feel at home___ with you.
That's why___ I feel at home___ with you.

you.___
you.___

You Took Advantage of Me

Gracefully

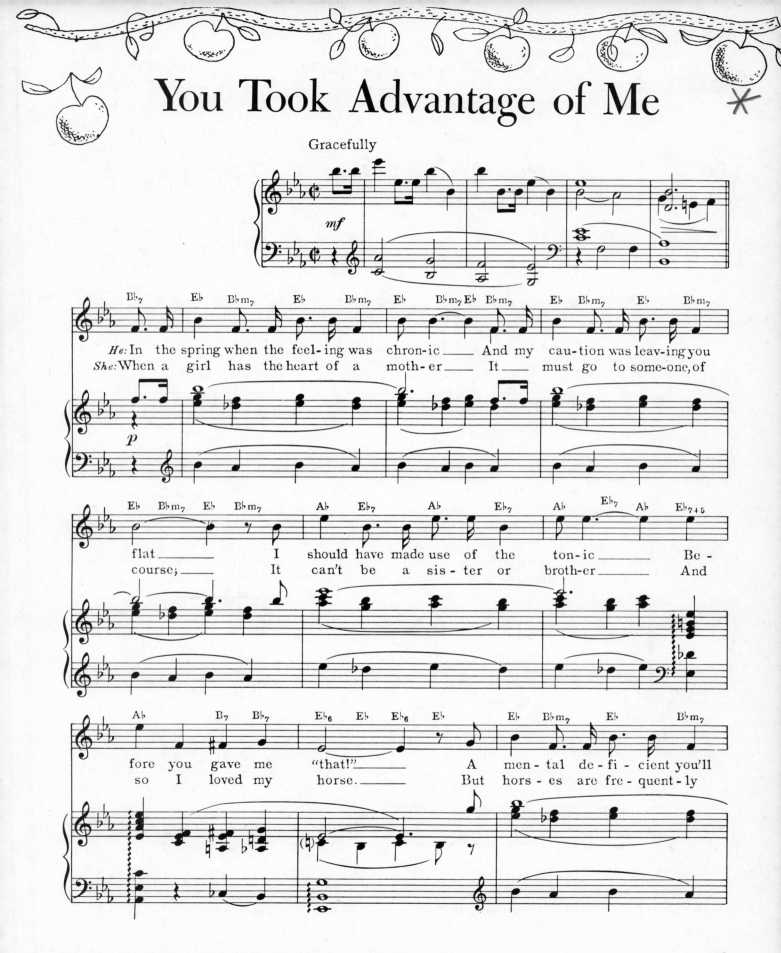

PART TWO
1929-1935

Spring Is Here

BY THE time *Spring Is Here* opened in 1929, Rodgers & Hart were celebrities. Reporters had begun to follow them around on their semi-annual jaunts to the Continent. Richard Rodgers no longer had to struggle with the newspapers to keep the "d" in his name. And stories began to be told about the way diminutive Larry Hart got folded up in upper berths and put away by porters who didn't know he was there.

People began to ask them, "Which comes first, the music or the lyrics?" and they had only begun to answer that sometimes it was one and sometimes the other—they would be answering that one for the next fourteen years. The most inquisitive people wanted to know how they worked together, and Rodgers playfully told a Philadelphia reporter: "It is practically impossible to start him working, but it is a feat of genius to make him stop once he has begun. He has never been known to show up for morning rehearsals, but the moment we start through the stage door for lunch, there is Larry breathlessly rushing in."

Hart chewed his cigar and told the same reporter: "The easiest way to send him into a rage is for me to say the orchestra is too loud. He doesn't want it to play too loudly, but he never thinks it is playing too loudly. And I know it is." Rodgers & Hart were good copy in 1929. The country was riding high, and Shipwreck Kelly perched on his flagpole made a nice vignette of the times.

Spring Is Here was about as serious as a Yale Derby Day. John Anderson, in the New York *Evening Journal,* commented that it provided "the only instance of musical comedy where the heroine falls before the final curtain does."

Heads Up

A SHIP WITHOUT A SAIL made its bow in *Heads Up,* which ran later in the same year. In this show Victor Moore, a veteran even then (he had begun back in 1894), idled away the hours in a ship's galley by inventing things. One of his prize inventions was a fluid to kill flies. "Does it work?" someone asked him. "Well, no," he said. "But it mixes nicely with ginger ale."

Writing in *The World,* Frank Sullivan commented that "A Ship without a Sail" was the best song since "Old Man River." In writing it Rodgers coolly ignored one of the cardinal rules of popular song writing which holds that a song should have a first theme consisting of eight measures. The first theme of "A Ship without a Sail" runs for twelve, and Rodgers has arranged the rest of the song accordingly. But he has done it so well that only the most careful observer has ever noticed it.

Simple Simon

A FEW MONTHS later Flo Ziegfeld had a good idea. It was simply to build a show around Ed Wynn, on the theory that three solid hours of The Perfect Fool would guarantee a success.

The idea turned out very well. Wynn laughed his infectious laugh and lay flat on his back on the stage to insist that business was looking up. He thereby contributed at least as much to the economic revival of the country as the people who were insisting in the fall of 1930 that miniature golf would become a big industry and save the country.

The characters in the show were divided into two groups, laughter-loving people (all wets recognized them as wets) and killjoys (all wets recognized them as drys). One well-known wet, Al Capone, enjoyed the show in Chicago, escorted by eighteen young bootleggers in dinner jackets which bulged slightly under the left arm.

The show included one simple-minded sequence in which Wynn emerged from the forest into a little clearing, spread a tablecloth on the ground, laid a duck and a ham on the cloth, and repeated delightedly to himself, "I love the woods, I love the woods." People of middle vintage will remember that this phrase became a rage. In retrospect, there doesn't seem to have been much reason for it, except possibly that the depression was making the woods look pretty good to city dwellers.

In the midst of all this, a girl named Ruth Etting (who joined the company twenty-four hours before the New York opening), stopped the show with "Ten Cents a Dance" (which Rodgers & Hart had written to order in three quarters of an hour). The beautiful, relaxed feeling of "Ten Cents a Dance" was just what was needed to distract the tired businessman, who was especially tired in 1930.

Evergreen

Dancing on the ceiling appeared in the fall of the year in a London show called *Evergreen*. It was danced and sung by Jessie Matthews on a set made to look like a ceiling with a big chandelier rising in the middle of the stage. The song did well in London, but it had a hard time getting started back home. Thrown out of *Simple Simon* in its original version, it was later banned for a long time by the radio networks. Although Rodgers and Hart tried hard to find out why, the closest they could get to an answer was that the use of the word "bed" in the song (see verse) was looked upon rather dubiously in some quarters. It is probably one of the most innocuous uses of the word ever made in a popular song with the possible exception of "Go to bed, you sleepyhead." The song caught on slowly but became a long-term hit.

*America's
Sweetheart*

In 1931 it was hard to get people to watch a show. Idle streets were lined with apple salesmen, and Hoovervilles were growing up in vacant lots. But when producers presented a show with songs by Rodgers & Hart like "I've Got Five Dollars" and an evening of Harriet Lake (known later as Ann Sothern), people still blew themselves to a show.

"I've Got Five Dollars" was the perfect Depression song. It had a short repetitive melody designed to suggest the itemized list of the two kids' assets. A song about five dollars wouldn't have meant much to an audience a few years before. But in 1931 a lot of people were taking inventory.

RODGERS AND HART went to Hollywood for the first time in 1930 and could be found there off and on for the next seven years, or until what Rodgers called their "pardon" from California, "a few short years ahead of Mooney." Hart didn't like it much either. "No one ever heard of movie writers. Who are the writers?" he snorted. "The fans think the actors make up the dialogue as they go along."

Love Me Tonight

Bᴜᴛ they did like making the Maurice Chevalier-Jeanette MacDonald picture, *Love Me Tonight*. It was about a French tailor who fell in love with a princess. Chevalier had a chance to wear his traditional costume, the ragged cap worn almost vertically and the turtle-neck sweater. Except for a putty nose, it was the same costume he had started out with in the Paris of World War I, singing "How Ya Gonna Keep Them Down on the Farm."

The charm of the Gallic twinkle and the Chevalier accent weren't lost on American audiences, in spite of a build-up which advertised a Chevalier who "loves like an Apache." Anybody who went to hear him sing "Mimi" and "Isn't It Romantic" like an Apache got quite a surprise.

"Lover," written for this movie, is a good example of the versatility and staying power of Rodgers & Hart songs. One of the most frequently heard Rodgers & Hart waltzes, it was played recently in an orchestral arrangement by the New York Philharmonic Orchestra.

Hallelujah, I'm a Bum

Hᴀʟʟᴇʟᴜᴊᴀʜ, ɪ'ᴍ ᴀ ʙᴜᴍ was a picture, naturally enough about bums, the leading bum being Al Jolson, the grand old man of talkies. In this movie Rodgers and Hart experimented with a technique called rhythmic dialogue, which required Jolson to sing not only his songs but his lines. Since much of the singing dialogue was written in Lorenz Hart rhyme, it had its bright spots, but *Hallelujah* turned out to be more experimental than successful. Its biggest song, "You Are Too Beautiful," survived by itself.

"Blue Moon" is unique as the only Rodgers & Hart song published not as a part of a show or movie score, but as a popular song. It was written originally for a Jean Harlow picture, with the title "Oh, Lord, Why Won't You Make Me a Star?" and was cut out of the picture. Renamed "The Bad in Every Man," it was cut out again. Orphaned once more, it was renamed "Blue Moon" and went out into the cold world where it made its own way very nicely.

With a Song in My Heart

Lively

mp

p

He: Though I know that we meet ev - 'ry night; And we
She: Oh, the moon's not a moon for a night; And these

E♭   E♭m7   E♭7

could - n't have changed since the last time, To my joy and de-light it's a
stars will not twin - kle and fade out! And the words in my ears will re-

A♭   E♭   Cm

new kind of love at first sight._____ Though it's you and it's I all the
sound for the rest of my years._____ In the morn-ing I'll find with de-

Fm7   B♭7   E♭ A♭   E♭ A♭   E♭

p

Can I help but re - joice_____ That a song such as
ours came to be? But I al-ways knew_____ I would live life
through_____ With a song in my heart for you.
you.

95

Yours Sincerely

Brightly

He: Dear-est one: I write what I'm a-fraid to speak; I'm
She: Do not think I have-n't got the heart to care; But

weak when I'm with you.
where is my ro-mance?

Tears of love are caus-ing all the ink to blot, So
So I've wait-ed for my lov-er to ap-pear, I

what am I to do?_____
fear, you've not a chance._____

Hop-ing to find the phras-es, Grop-ing to find each
I must con-fess I've found one, You must re-call, last

word, How they all burned like blaz-es!
night, Tru-ly it does as-tound one

Now they all sound ab-surd. Though I don't know
How two can love at sight. But I like your

97

breath a - way. Ver - y tru - ly___ my pas - sion is un - ru - ly.___ A dream of you is new - ly born each night and day. Oh, but my thoughts are fer - vent! How can I make them

plain? Ev-er your hum-ble ser-vant Faith-ful-ly I re-main. I'm in-tend-ing___ To find a hap-py end-ing___ Be-cause I love you dear-ly. I'm sin-cere-ly yours!___ yours!___

A Ship without a Sail

Moderately slow tempo

mf poco a poco cresc.

rall.

He: I don't know what day it is, Or if it's dark or fair; Some-
She: When love leaves you all a-lone, You're liv-ing in the past;

molto legato
mp a tempo

how, that's just the way it is, And I don't real-ly
Then you feel so small a-lone, And oh! the world seems

mf

care. _____
vast. _____

I go to this or that place, I
You tell your grief to no girls, You

seem a - live and well; My head is just a hat place, My
nev - er make it known; Your smile is like a show-girl's, Your

breast an emp - ty shell! _____ And I've a
laugh a hol. - low tone. _____ And then your

fad - ed dream to sell. _____
lit - tle heart's a stone. _____

102

Refrain (not fast)

All a-lone, all at sea! Why does no-bod-y care for me,

When there's no love to hold my love? Why is my heart so frail,

Like a ship with-out a sail?_____ Out on the o-cean,

sail-ors can use a chart;_____ I'm on the o-cean guid-ed by just a

lone - - ly heart. Still a - lone, still at sea!

Still there's no one to care for me When there's no hand to hold my hand.

Life is a love - less tale For a ship with - out a

sail. sail.

Ten Cents a Dance

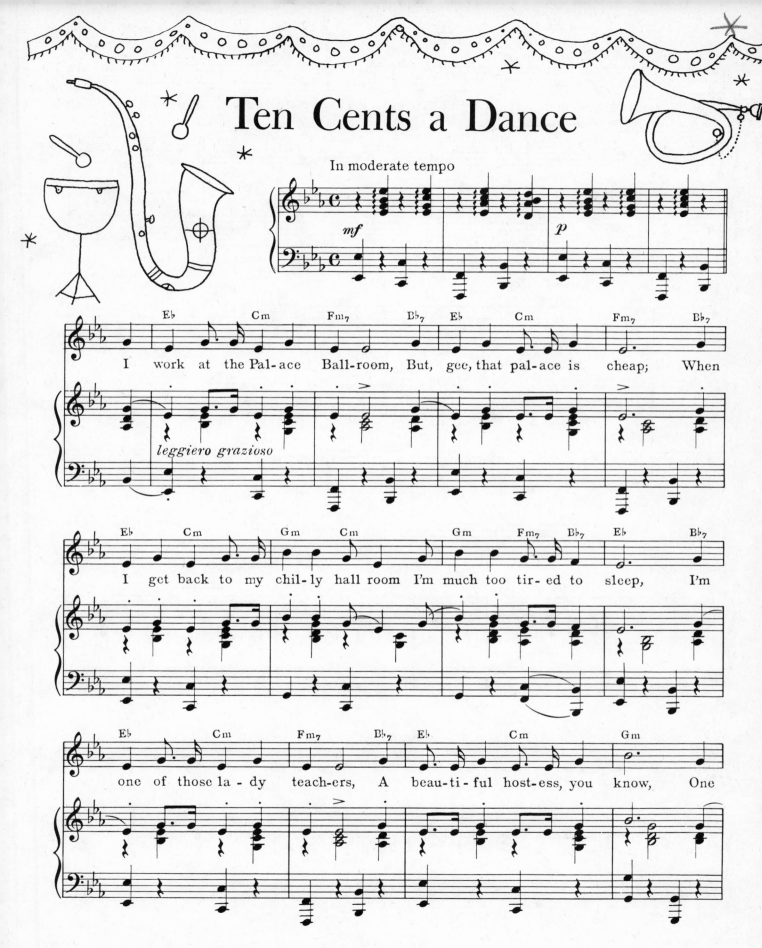

In moderate tempo

I work at the Pal-ace Ball-room, But, gee, that pal-ace is cheap; When

I get back to my chil-ly hall room I'm much too tir-ed to sleep, I'm

one of those la-dy teach-ers, A beau-ti-ful host-ess, you know, One

that the pal-ace fea-tures At ex-act-ly a dime a throw.

poco rit.

Refrain (slowly, quasi rubato)

Ten cents a dance; That's what they pay me. Gosh, how they weigh me

down! Ten cents a dance, Pan-sies and rough guys,

Tough guys who tear my gown! Sev-en to mid-night, I hear drums,

PATTER

Fight-ers and sail-ors and bow-leg-ged tai-lors Can pay for their tick-ets and rent me! Butch-ers and bar-bers and rats from the har-bors Are sweet-hearts my good luck has sent me. Though I've a cho-rus of el-der-ly beaux, Stock-ings are por-ous with holes at the toes.

Dancing on the Ceiling

The world is lyr - i - cal

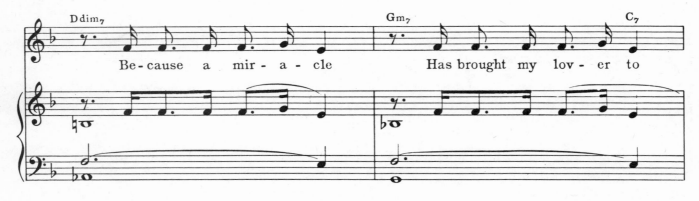

Be - cause a mir - a - cle Has brought my lov - er to

me! Though he's some oth - er place, His

I whis-per "Go a-way, my lov-er, It's not fair,"___

But I'm so grate-ful to dis-cov-er He's still there.___

I love my ceil-ing more Since it is a danc-ing floor Just for___

___ my love.___ love.___

I've Got Five Dollars

He: Mis - ter Shy - lock was stin - gy; ___ I was mis - er - ly,
She: Peg - gy Joyce has a bus' - ness, ___ All her hus - bands have

too. I was more self - ish and crab - by than a shell-fish,
gold. And Lil - yan Tash-man is not kissed by an ash-man;

Oh dear,— it's queer— What love— can do!
But now,— some-how— Wealth leaves me cold.

I'd give all— my pos-ses-sions for you:_____
Though you're poor as a church mouse I'm sold!_____

Refrain (leisurely)

He: I've got five dol-lars; I'm in good con-
She: I've got five dol-lars; Eight-y five re-

di-tion; And I've got am - bi-tion; That be-longs to
la-tions; Two lace com-bi - na-tions; They be-long to

you; Six shirts and col-lars; Debts be - yond en -
you! Two coats with col-lars; Ma and Grand-ma

dur-ance On my life in - sur-ance, That be-longs to
wore 'em; All the moths a - dore 'em; They be-long to

you; _____ I've got a heart That
you; _____ I've got two lips That

mp dolce

must be spurt-in'! Just be cer - tain
care for mat - ing, There-fore wait - ing

I'll be true!
will not do!

Take my five dol-lars!
Take my five dol-lars!

Take my shirts and col-lars!
Take my coats and col-lars!

Take my heart that hol-lers,
Take my heart that hol-lers,

"Ev-'ry-thing I've got be-longs to you!"
"Ev-'ry-thing I've got be-longs to you!"

you!"
you!"

Lover

Moderate waltz tempo

When you held your hand to my heart, Dear, you did some-thing grand to my heart, And we played the scene to per-fec-tion, _____ Though we did-n't have the

118

eyes, _____ Till Love's__ own en-tranc - ing__ mu - sic
bliss, _____ When two__ lips of cor - al__ want to

dies. _____ All of my fu-ture is
kiss? _____ I say "The Dev-il is

in you. _____ Your ev - 'ry plan I de - sign _____
in you." _____ And to re - sist you I try; _____

Prom-ise you'll al- ways con - tin - ue _____ to be mine. _____
But if you did- n't con - tin - ue _____ I would die! _____

Mimi

Very gaily, but in moderate tempo

My left shoe's on my right foot, My right shoe's on my left. Oh!
lis - ten to me Mi - mi, Of rea - son I'm be - reft! The
but-tons of my trou-sers Are but-ton'd to my vest; Oh! lis - ten to me

Mi-mi, You've got me sad and dream-y,

You could free me, If you'd see me, Mi-mi,

You know I'd like to have a lit-tle son of a Mi-mi bye and

bye.

bye.

Isn't It Romantic?

I've nev-er met you, Yet nev-er
My face is glow-ing, I'm en-er-

doubt, dear, I can't for-get you, I've thought you out dear, I know your
get-ic, The art of sew-ing, I found po-et-ic, My nee-dle

pro-file and I know the way you kiss just the thing I
punc-tu-ates the rhy-thm of ro-mance! I don't give a

miss on a night like this. If dreams are made of im-ag-i-
stitch, if I don't get rich. A cus-tom tai-lor who has no

na-tion, I'm not a-fraid of my own cre-a-tion. With all my
cus-tom, Is like a sail-or, no one will trust 'em. But there is

heart, my heart is here for you to take. Why should I quake? I'm not a-wake.
mag-ic in the mu-sic of my shears; I shed no tears. Lend me your ears!

Refrain (with simplicity)

Is-n't it ro-man-tic? Mu-sic in the night, A dream that can be
Is-n't it ro-man-tic? Soon I will have found some girl that I a-

such a night as this? Is-n't it ro-man-tic? Ev-'ry note that's sung is
cook me on-ion soup. Kid-dies are ro-man-tic, And if we don't fight, we

like a lov-er's kiss. Sweet sym-bols in the moon-light,
soon will have a troupe! We'll help the pop-u-la-tion,

Do you mean that I will fall in love per-chance?___ Is-n't it ro-
It's a du-ty that we owe to dear old France.___ Is-n't it ro-

mance? Is-n't it ro-mance?___

You Are Too Beautiful

Like all fools, I be- lieved what I want- ed to be- lieve, My fool- ish heart con- ceived what fool- ish hearts con- ceive. I thought I found a mir- a- cle, I

Blue Moon

Calmly

Once up-on a time, be-fore I took up smil-ing, I hat-ed the moon-light!
Once up-on a time My heart was just an or-gan, My life had no mis-sion.

Shad-ows of the night that po-ets find be-guil-ing seemed
Now that I have you, to be as rich as Mor-gan is

flat as the moon-light.
my one am-bi-tion.

With no one to stay
Once I a-woke at

PART THREE
1935-1938

Jumbo
On Your Toes
Babes in Arms
I'd Rather Be Right
I Married an Angel

Jumbo

EVERY Saturday from Labor Day until November 16, people wondered whether it would be safe to go away for the week end. Nobody wanted to miss *Jumbo*, and nobody, not even Billy Rose, could be sure when it was going to open. Rose hung a big sign on the boarded-up Hippodrome saying, "SH-H-H, *Jumbo* is rehearsing," and since Actor's Equity had classified it as a circus, not a show, he was able to rehearse the show until he had what he wanted, which took three months.

Rose's publicity men began working late, too. They took Big Rosie, the show's elephant, to Brooklyn, parked her outside a school, and went in to get the kids. But they came out to find her eating a barrel of tar, and since she was the only elephant they had and absolutely invaluable, they never did this again. Rose offered a private preview of *Jumbo* to anyone who thought it was worth ten thousand dollars, and a whisky distiller got as far as preliminary negotiations. There was so much speculation about *Jumbo's* debut that Billy Rose finally bought space in the papers: "I'll be a dirty name," he said, "if I'll open *Jumbo* until it's ready," and when it finally opened, *The New Yorker* cracked, "Well, they finally got *Jumbo* into the Hippodrome last Saturday night. Now all that remains is to complete the Triborough Bridge and enforce the sanctions against Italy."

Jumbo was an adventure in theatrical engineering. Even the tickets were nine times the ordinary size. Backed by such reliables as John Hay Whitney and Herbert Bayard Swope, it featured Rodgers & Hart, Ben Hecht and Charles MacArthur, Jimmy Durante, Paul Whiteman, and a thousand animals. It was rehearsed not only in the Hippodrome but in unrelated units from Central Park to Canarsie, and the stage manager almost gave up in despair when he came to a stage instruction reading, "Exit an elephant." Even dauntless Billy Rose complained, "How was I to know there was a timeless feud between the water buffaloes and the alpacas?"

Jumbo was a show about a war between two rival circuses. As the ads said, there was ONLY ONE RING TO WATCH, and in that ring there appeared a forty-foot jack-in-the-box, a pair of acrobats who did aerial stunts dangling on their toes from a speeding plane, a couple who balanced on a plank over an open cage of roaring lions, and a certain clown named A. Robins who made himself famous because bananas grew in his left coat pocket while he tried to play the violin. *Jumbo* was the biggest sensation in the Hippodrome since 1905 when sixty-four young women with heads high and eyes front had marched stoically down a long stairway into a tankful of water seventeen feet deep and never came out again. (A note had been inserted in the program by the Shuberts which read: "No apprehension need be felt that anyone disappearing in the tank is in danger.")

Jumbo was the first Broadway show with Rodgers & Hart songs since 1931, and they were fresh, straightforward songs in sharp contrast to *Jumbo's* razzle-dazzle and ballyhoo. Rodgers was once more tampering with convention. "My Romance" and "Little Girl Blue" both violated the 32-measure tradition which broke a melody up into sections of 8 measures and required the main theme to be repeated before the "bridge." And the lyrics were studded with the triple rhymes for which Hart was famous.

On Your Toes

THE story of *On Your Toes* began in Hollywood when a studio turned down a two-page scenario because it didn't give Astaire a chance to wear a top hat. Rodgers & Hart met Lee Shubert on the street a few days later and told him about it. Shubert was looking for a show for non-top-hatted Ray Bolger and took an option on the scenario, but let it lapse. Finally Dwight Deere Wiman bought it, Bolger was signed, and Monty Woolley decided to try acting. The show opened April 11, and at Christmas-time it was still hard to get seats for a matinee. It was so successful that the movies couldn't afford to let it go by, and finally bought it for a sum considerably rounder than the one they had been quoted in 1935.

On Your Toes was about the ballet (just beginning its tremendous vogue in this country), the WPA (a large government organization), and racketeers (the only people working overtime). It kidded the classical ballet and introduced a style of its own—the unforgettable *Slaughter on Tenth Avenue*. Veteran showmen shook their heads and forecast that *Slaughter on Tenth Avenue* would be suicide on Broadway. People, they said, didn't go to musicals to be reminded of gang warfare; Dillinger was only two years in his grave, Bruno Hauptmann was awaiting execution, and small boys all over the country were playing cops and robbers with convincing imitations of submachine guns.

But Rodgers & Hart were convinced once again that the only thing that was murder at the box office was something that had been done before. Producers began to realize that musicals would be more and not less attractive to the public if they concerned themselves with the life led outside the theatre. A musical could do more to ease the cares of the day if it handled the cares irreverently than it could if it never touched them at all.

The people who went to *On Your Toes* heard a new kind of score. Before the Rodgers & Hart shows of the thirties, musicals usually consisted of a book and some good songs the composer had written, and the songs were superimposed over the book or the book inserted around the songs. If the song writers had a good novelty song, they made a

141

place for it. If the book called for a love song, they wrote a love song, but no one looked to see whether it was the type of song the hero would be likely to sing, being a particular guy in a particular situation.

In Rodgers & Hart shows, the songs were written to fit the requirements of the story, the role of the singer, and the general character of the rest of the score. "There's a Small Hotel," sung by naïve, unsophisticated people, has no complicated rhythms or tricky rhymes. A homogeneous show instead of a collection of parts, the musical was coming of age.

Babes in Arms

Babes in arms was a kids' show, written about children and for child stars; as one wag said, there was hardly a legal drinker in the cast. Opening night was the event of the year for talent scouts. There was a young singer named Alfred Drake; a one-hundred-fifty-pound fifteen-year-old fresh from a church choir in Pennsylvania, Wynn Murray, who sang "Johnny One Note" so that no one in the second balcony missed a word; and a seventeen-year-old Mitzi Green with a big rectangular smile and a wonderful song called "The Lady Is a Tramp."

All the young faces made Benchley think of the *Garrick Gaieties*: "Several years ago," he wrote in *The New Yorker*, "when all the world (except Justices McReynolds, Van Devanter, Sutherland, and Butler) was young, the song-writing team of Rodgers & Hart emerged as forces in the international scene with a noisy gang of youngsters their own age." Now twelve years later they emerged again with a new gang of youngsters.

Rodgers & Hart wrote *Babes in Arms* with the idea that audiences would appreciate some new faces. In many weeks of casting during the summer of 1936, they saw five thousand hopefuls, most of whom seemed deeply impressed by Zasu Pitts, Mae West, or W. C. Fields. It

142

was hard to find young performers who had developed styles of their own.

The show cost only fifty-five thousand dollars to stage. Since most of it was supposed to be an amateur revue put on by kids, there was no elaborate scenery, or costumes—the Egyptian scene was done with bath towels.

But there were plenty of songs. Both "The Lady Is a Tramp" and "Where or When" were slow starters, picking up speed as the show grew older. Larry Hart wrote two extra verses for "The Lady Is a Tramp," and the copyright owners labeled it "special material" which could not be quoted. "I Wish I Were in Love Again" had the kind of quotable lyrics which appealed to all the slightly disenchanted (which at one time or another is practically everybody), and Mitzi Green launched the mild-mannered love song "My Funny Valentine" in a simple, unaffected way that was unforgettable.

The popular "Johnny One Note" was anything but orthodox and suggested much of the development to come in Rodgers' songs. The emphatic hard-hitting rhythms were a long way from the bouncy songs like "Manhattan." And Hart's lyrics were not the virtuoso performances they had been ten years before—they said more than they had before. Letters came in from all over the country saying that the writers had had experiences like the one described in "Where or When."

But *Babes in Arms* was an experience no one had had before. It's still one of Rodgers' favorites.

I'd Rather Be Right

DURING the season of 1937-1938 it took a show like *I'd Rather Be Right* to lure audiences away from their copies of *Gone with the Wind*. Walter P. Chrysler heard so much about the show that he offered a 1938 coupé for four good seats, and some eager first-nighters paid a hundred dollars to see what had happened to President Roosevelt in the hands of George S. Kaufman and Moss Hart (no relation to Larry), the team

143

that had written *You Can't Take It with You* a year before. There was some gossip about what "they" would do about a show that lampooned the President, but George M. Cohan made such a likable FDR ("Cummings, take a law,") that it looked as if he could wangle a third term, if FDR couldn't.

Jim Farley, Frances Perkins, and Henry Morgenthau got the worst of it. Eleanor Roosevelt was graciously left out. Mr. Farley informed the President that the chairman of the fourth assembly district in Seattle wanted to be Collector of the Port of New York. "But we've got a Collector of the Port of New York," said FDR. "Not in Seattle," Mr. Farley assured him.

In November, 1937, the only two musicals on Broadway were Rodgers & Hart shows—*Babes in Arms* and *I'd Rather Be Right*. As fast as they were productive, Rodgers & Hart wrote the score for *I'd Rather Be Right* in a month, working mainly on the Superchief and in a booth at Sardi's, with occasional flights to Long Island and Central Park West.

The tune people liked best was the sentimental "Have You Met Miss Jones?," a modest little song that wasn't expected to place at all. It has a daring middle section with rapid modulations from one key to another which are quite a challenge to the bathtub singer.

I Married an Angel

I MARRIED AN ANGEL had a complicated history. Originally a Hungarian play, it was bought by MGM in 1933. Moss Hart, Rodgers, and Hart did a treatment of it for the films. Then the script began to collect dust in the MGM cupboard. Rodgers & Hart persuaded Dwight Deere Wiman to buy it, and Wiman produced it in 1938 as the third in an annual series of Rodgers & Hart spring musicals. MGM then bought it back and made a movie of it. Rodgers & Hart got paid for the show after each transaction—as a script, a show, and a movie.

Zorina, the Norwegian danseuse who had her first important role in *I Married an Angel,* caused a little controversy and a lot of admiration.

When the show was ready to be cast, Wiman told Rodgers about a girl in the London company of *On Your Toes* who should have a small part in the show. Rodgers told him they weren't making places for anyone—the show would have as many dancers as it needed and no more. A few months later Rodgers went to a party in California where he met Zorina. He wired Wiman: "Have just met Zorina. Small part nothing." She played the angel.

I Married an Angel was a smash hit, but before the opening Rodgers & Hart had the usual qualms about it. Rodgers said later: "The awful thing about an opening night is that you can't trust anyone or anything to supply you with an accurate indication as to the success or failure of a show. It's madness to listen to people since they are invariably the victims of wish fulfillment, hoping it will be good or bad, depending entirely on their personal attitude toward you. After hearing ultimate failures cheered passionately on opening night and seeing great successes received with complete coldness, you can't even trust the evidence of your own ears. I was badly confused the night *I Married an Angel* opened. I was sure the audience didn't like it, and I said so. It took great reviews in the papers and weeks of capacity business to convince me."

"Spring Is Here," a not-too-sad lament, was sung by Dennis King and Vivienne Segal. And the title song, first sung by Dennis King, was used to advantage by a lot of husbands around the country.

Little Girl Blue

Moderately bright

mf dim. e rit.

not fast

Sit there and count your fin-gers, what can you do? Old girl, you're

p a tempo

through. Sit there and count your lit-tle fin-gers, Un-

luck-y lit-tle girl blue. _____ Sit there and

mf   *p*

count the rain-drops fall-ing on you. It's time you knew, all you can count on is the rain-drops That fall on lit-tle girl blue._____ No use, old girl, you may as well sur - ren-der, Your hope is get-ting slen-der, Why

The cir-cus tent was strung_____ with ev-'ry star in the

sky A - bove the ring_____ I loved so well;_____

Now the young world has grown old,_____

Gone are the tin-sel and gold._____

D.S. al Fine 𝄋

149

My Romance

Moderately

mf

poco rit.

p a tempo

Em6 D7 Em6 D7 Em6 D7 Em6 D7

I won't kiss your hand, Ma - dam, Cra - zy for you though I am.

G7 C7 F Fm C G7 C

I'll nev-er woo you on bend-ed knee, No Ma-dam, not me.

Em6 D7 Em6 D7 G Dm7 G7

We don't need that flow-'ry fuss, No sir, Ma-dam, not for us.

The Most Beautiful Girl in the World

Moderate Waltz tempo

We used to spend the spring to-geth-er be-fore we learned to walk; _____ We used to laugh and sing to-geth-er be-fore we learned how to talk. _____

With no rea - son for the sea - son

Spring would end as it would start.____

Now the sea - son has a rea - son, And there's spring-time in my heart.____

Guitar tacet

154

who can make me be - lieve it's a beau-ti-ful world.

So - cial ___ not a bit, _____ Nat - 'ral ___ kind of

wit, _____ She'd shine ___ an - y - where _____ And she

has-n't got plat-i-num hair _____ The most beau-ti-ful house in the

There's a Small Hotel

Moderately bright

mp

poco rit.

Am7   F#   G   Am7   F#

She: I'd like to get a - way, Jun-ior, Some-where a - lone with

p a tempo

G   Am7   D7   F#   Am7   D7

you.   It could be oh, so gay, Jun-ior! You need a laugh or

G   Am7   F#   G

two.   *He:* A cer-tain place I know, Frank-ie,

When the stee-ple bell says "Good - night, sleep well," we'll

thank the small ho - tel to - geth - er. ____

1.

2. tel. ____ We'll creep in - to our lit - tle shell ____ And we will

poco a poco cresc.

thank the small ho - tel to - geth - er. ____

rit.

L.H. mf

Ped.

Where or When?

In moderate tempo

mp

slowly Cm₇ ... When you're a-wake the things you think come from the dreams you

dream. Thought has wings, And lots of things are sel-dom what they

seem. Some-times you think you've lived be - fore

All that you live to-day. Things you do_____ come back to you, _____ As though they knew the way. Oh, the tricks your mind can play!

Refrain (slowly, with very much sentiment)

It seems we stood and talked like this be-fore, We looked at each oth-er in the same way then, But I can't re-mem-ber where or

The Lady Is a Tramp

In strict tempo

I've wined and dined on mul-li-gan stew and never wished for tur-key, As I hitched and hiked and grift-ed too from Maine to Al-bu-quer-que.____ A-

la-dy   is   a   tramp.

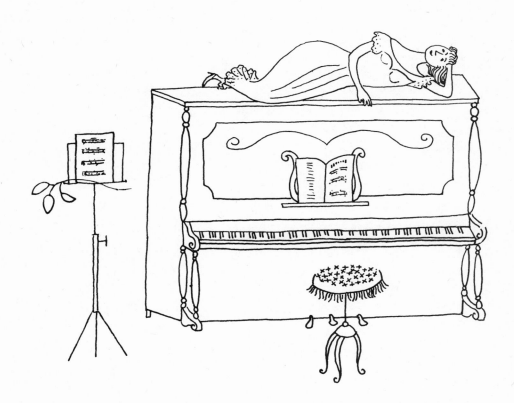

My Funny Valentine

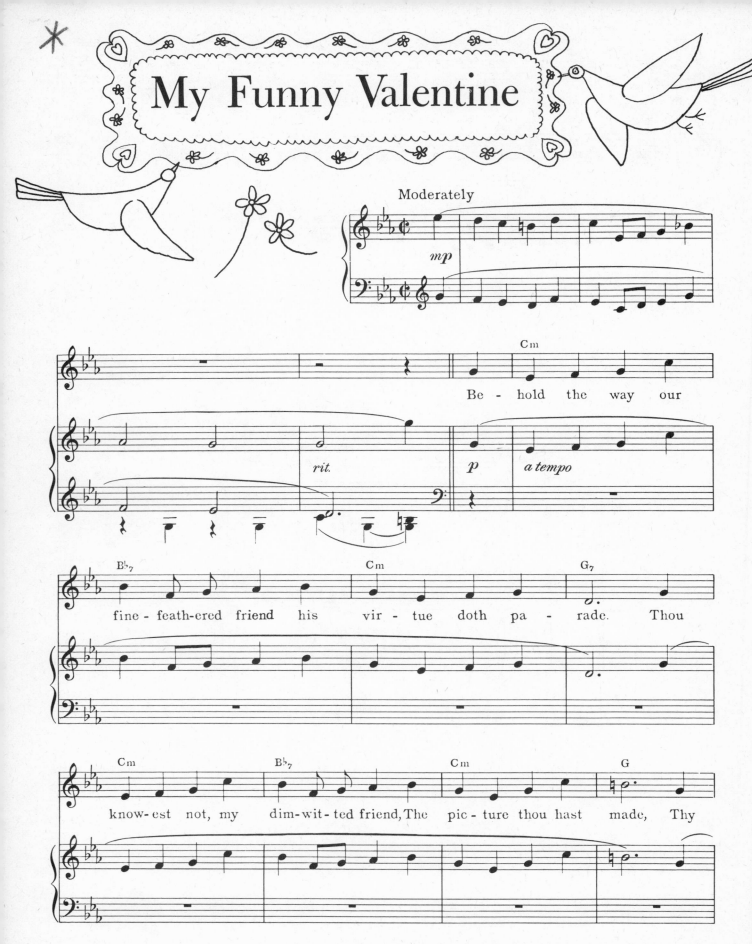

va - cant brow and thy tous - led hair con - ceal thy good in - tent. Thou

no - ble, up - right, truth - ful, sin - cere and slight - ly dop - ey gent, you're

Refrain (slowly, with much expression)

My fun - ny Val - en - tine, Sweet com - ic Val - en - tine,

You make me smile with my heart. _____

Your looks are laugh - a - ble, Un - pho - to - graph - a - ble,

Yet you're my fav - 'rite work of art. _____ Is your

fig - ure less than Greek; Is your mouth a lit - tle weak, when you

o - pen it to speak, Are you smart? _____ But

don't change a hair for me, Not if you care for me,

Stay, lit - tle Val - en - tine, stay!

Each day is Val - en - tine's day.

day.

Johnny One Note

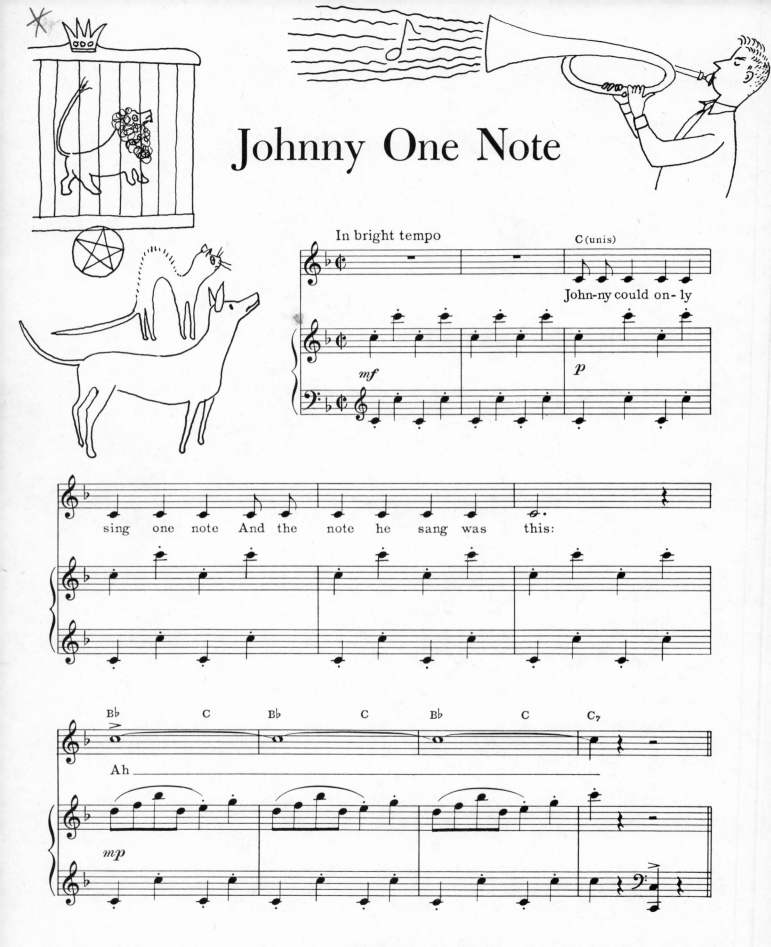

In bright tempo

John-ny could on- ly sing one note And the note he sang was this: Ah

flute _____ or the big trom - bone _____ Ev - 'ry-one was

mute, _____ John - ny stood a - lone.

TRIO

Cats and dogs stopped yap - ping, Li - ons in the zoo all _ were

jeal - ous _ of John - ny's _ big trill. _____

Have You Met Miss Jones?

me. _____ Then I said, "Miss Jones, You're a girl who un-der-stands I'm a man who must be free."_____ And all at once I lost my breath, And all at once was scared to death, And all at once I owned the

earth and sky!_____ Now I've met Miss

Jones,   And we'll keep on meet- ing till we die,_____

_____ Miss Jones and I.

1.

2. I._____

Spring Is Here

Quietly

mf

poco rit.

p a tempo

Once there was a thing called spring, when the world was writ-ing vers-es like yours and mine All the lads and girls would sing, When we sat at lit-tle ta-bles and drank May wine.

Now A - pril, May and June are sad - ly out of tune

Life has stuck the pin in the bal - loon.

Refrain (slowly, with expression)

Spring is here! Why does - n't my heart go danc-ing?

Spring is here! Why is - n't the waltz en-

pear Why does-n't the night in - vite me?

May - be it's be - cause no-bod - y loves

me, Spring is here I hear!

hear!

I Married an Angel

Moderately

mf

calmly

There's been a change in me! I have a love-ly dis-po-

p semplice

si-tion, That's ver-y strange in me. And life's as sweet as it can be.

I've lots of cour-age and am-bi-tion.___ From ev-'ry care my mind is free,

PART FOUR
1938-1942

The Boys from Syracuse
Too Many Girls
Higher and Higher
Pal Joey
By Jupiter

The Boys from Syracuse

RODGERS & HART decided to do a Shakespearean musical while on the train to Atlantic City, where they were going to work on *I Married an Angel*. Starting from their principle that the unsafest thing to do commercially is the only safe thing, they agreed Shakespeare was their most unlikely choice and provided the freshest material. Before the train was in, they had decided on *A Comedy of Errors* and cast Jimmy Savo and Teddy Hart, Larry's brother, as the twin Dromios. It was the first time anyone had made a musical out of Shakespeare.

The only Shakespeare left intact in this robust musical was the line, "The venom clamours of a jealous woman poisons more deadly than a mad dog's tooth." Nobody felt he could sharpen this one, and in a script which consisted mainly of Greek gentlemen getting into beds not their own, the line had wide application. Beyond this the Bard would have had to look closely to see traces of his *A Comedy of Errors*, and Old Plautus, from whom Shakespeare lifted the story, would have found it an entirely new experience.

Teddy Hart had to have his heels built up to measure up to Jimmy Savo's five feet two, but with this done it was hard to tell them apart. Rodgers & Hart chose Eddie Albert and Marcy Wescott to sing "This Can't Be Love," and Wynn Murray, the outsized star of *Babes in Arms*, was signed to lope across the stage after Jimmy Savo. It was Rodgers' and Hart's twenty-fifth show together and such a success that Garson Kanin wrote Rodgers after the show opened saying they had better watch out for the antitrust laws.

Richard Rodgers has a theory that people like waltz time better than any other meter, and one of his most popular waltzes is still "Falling in Love with Love." It was a success from the moment Muriel Angelus first sang it.

Too
Many
Girls

As their string of successes lengthened, Rodgers & Hart braced themselves against the law of averages. And when the dress rehearsal of *Too Many Girls* went off very badly in New Haven, they were sure it had finally happened. But it hadn't. This rowdy show about college football in a place called Pottawatomie was pure pleasant entertainment, a welcome change from the newspaper headlines of October, 1939.

Again, the original story was written for the movies, this time by George Marion, Jr. Marion told Rodgers & Hart about it, and they took the idea to George Abbott. Marion liked working with Rodgers & Hart; he was much pleased with the whole arrangement. "They let me change my own lines," he said. "In Hollywood they ask the second assistant property man or the producer's half-sister's aunt. But the author is left severely alone in a corner. No one speaks to him. It is a social error to be caught having any conversation with him until the picture is finished."

Too Many Girls was mostly girls, with a few men to set them off. The story concerned one Consuelo Casey, whose millionaire father had $7150 more than Henry Ford. Consuelo, like too many girls at Pottawatomie, was prone to marry, and the show resounded with the loud mating cries of the female and the reluctant responses of the male.

Mary Jane Walsh led a mass attack on Manhattan with "Give It Back to the Indians," and Marcy Wescott had the best mating cry of all in the classic, "I Didn't Know What Time It Was."

Higher and Higher

OF *Higher and Higher* Richard Rodgers says, "When a trained seal steals the show, you know how bad it is." But this seal did happen to be a very unusual seal, with a penchant for attacking people from the rear.

The main trouble was that the show was originally designed for Zorina. When her picture commitments kept her in Hollywood, the show was rebuilt around a singing star, Marta Eggerth, wife of Jan Kiepura. She did all she could with a part that didn't jell. Rodgers & Hart never again redesigned a show if they couldn't get the cast they needed.

The show had its bright spots ("Yale is a period a lot of men go through between change of voice and selling insurance") but the best one was Shirley Ross singing the lazily mournful "It Never Entered My Mind."

Pal Joey

IT WAS John O'Hara's idea to make a musical out of Pal Joey. Early in 1940 he wrote Rodgers a letter. "Dear Dick: I don't know whether you happened to see any of a series of pieces I've been doing for *The New Yorker* in the past year or so. They're about a guy who is a master of ceremonies in cheap night clubs, and the pieces are in the form of letters from him to a successful band leader. Anyway I got the idea that the pieces, or at least the character and the life in general, could be made into a show, and I wonder if you and Larry would be interested in working on it with me. I read that you two have a commitment with Dwight Wiman for a show this spring, but if and when you get through with that I do hope you like my idea. Faithfully, John." Larry and Dick responded enthusiastically by return mail.

Pal Joey was not exactly conventional fare. The hero was a heel, the heroine a restless married lady who paid for her boy friends, the second male lead was not precisely the fellow you'd choose for your kid sister, and his girl friend wasn't far behind him. It was a lean, sardonic show, and the realism of the John O'Hara story was a strange new element in a musical. The show had a haunting power that affected people deeply; not many went away untouched by the combination of Larry Hart and John O'Hara.

Not a little of the show's power was due to a superb performance by a catlike Gene Kelly, who had been spotted by Rodgers & Hart when he played in Saroyan's *The Time of Your Life*. (Kelly worked his way through the University of Pittsburgh by running a dance studio.) The tough girl friend was June Havoc's first big role, and sister Gypsy Rose Lee went down to Philadelphia to see her opening night. No one could believe the next day that June had once been fired from a show for not being sexy enough. As *Time* put it, she "made a rhinestone gown twitch with significance."

"Bewitched" was written for Vivienne Segal who needed a torch-song, and Gene Kelly and Leila Ernst (who played the only nice person in the show) sang the sweet "I Could Write a Book." *Pal Joey* made history as the first musical to star our more unpleasant citizens.

By Jupiter

BY JUPITER was the last Rodgers & Hart show. They did a second version of *A Connecticut Yankee* in 1943, but September 6, 1942, was the twenty-seventh and last time they opened a new show together.

War had been declared eight months before. On September 5, the Germans reported gains in Stalingrad, and the Japanese landed reinforcements on Guadalcanal. Scenic designer Jo Mielziner went from *By Jupiter* into war camouflage, and director Joshua Logan just had time to finish the show before going into the army. *By Jupiter* ran a year and nine days, and a scant six weeks after it closed Larry Hart died of pneumonia in New York City, November 22, 1943.

His last show was a gay, careless one, an adaptation of *The Warrior's Husband,* the play that had made Katharine Hepburn famous eleven years before. It was about an amiable war between men and women, in this case a rather timid breed of Greek warriors and a brash race of Amazons. Ray Bolger in the old Romney Brent role was a reluctant warrior and Benay Venuta, queen of the Amazons, was his heroic queen-size wife. She had a sister, Constance Moore, who sang "Nobody's Heart" and was much admired by Ronald Graham in "Wait Till You See Her."

Like all shows, *By Jupiter* was full of high-grade problems at the last moment. Benay Venuta's eleven-month-old baby was stood up by a nurse who eloped with a sailor just before the opening. The title had to be changed (it was *All's Fair*), and there weren't enough funny lines. Ronald Graham was called in five days before the opening when the original lead didn't work into the part, and Constance Moore was covered with bruises from her dueling practice. Ray Bolger expressed the general fatigue when Constance Moore told him at a rehearsal to take a rest and stop dancing. "What's the use? I'll just get tired again."

By 1942, Rodgers & Hart had written over a thousand songs together and were the oldest working partnership in the theatre. Musical comedy had changed vastly since the days when they began. A musical was no longer the sum of its parts. It had a score instead of a collection of isolated song numbers and a book instead of a series of thinly related scenes. There was a family resemblance to all the material in a show, and the songs helped the book along instead of holding it up. This meant that the book itself had to be more substantial, and audiences that had once been satisfied to see the hero kiss the girl in the second act now required a little wit and imagination. Musical comedy, before and after Rodgers & Hart, was not the same at all.

By 1942, Broadway had also outgrown its old habit of comparing Rodgers & Hart to Gilbert & Sullivan. In the twenties, they had rivaled Gilbert & Sullivan; in the early thirties, they had been our own Gilbert & Sullivan. And then people forgot about comparing them to anybody. By this time, we knew Rodgers & Hart had made unique contributions to the American theatre.

Falling in Love with Love

Cut the thread, but leave _____ The whole heart whole. _____

Mer - ry maids can sew and sleep, Wives can on - ly sew and weep!

203

Learn-ing to trust is just For chil-dren in school. _____ I fell in love with love one night When the moon was full, _____ I was un-wise with eyes Un-a-ble to see. _____

This Can't Be Love

208

Give It Back to the Indians

Big bar - gain to - day, Chief, take__ it a - way!

Come, you bust-ed Cit - y slick - ers, Bet-ter take it on the chin.__

Fa -ther Knick has lost his knick - ers, Give it back to the In - - - di-

ans! ans!__

213

I Didn't Know What Time It Was

Moderately

mf · poco rit.

p a tempo

Once I was young, yes-ter-day, per-haps, Danced with Jim and Paul And kissed some oth-er chaps. Once I was young, but nev-er was na-ïve, I thought I had a trick or two up my im-ag-i-nar-y sleeve.

And now I know I was na - ïve!

Refrain (slowly and tenderly)

I did - n't know what time it was, Then I met you. Oh, what a love - ly time it was, How sub - lime it was, too! I did - n't

voice say I'm all your own! I ____ did-n't know what year it was,

Life ____ was no prize. I ____ want-ed love and here it was

Shin-ing out of your eyes. I'm wise ____ and I know what time it is

now! now! ____

It Never Entered My Mind

With tranquillity

I don't care if there's pow-der on my nose, I don't care if my hair-do is in place. I've lost the ver-y mean-ing of re-pose, I nev-er put a mud pack on my face. Oh, who'd have thought that I'd

Bewitched

Moderately

mf ... *poco rit.*

(not fast)

p a tempo

| Dm7 | G7 | Cmaj7 C6 | Dm7 | G7 | Cmaj7 | A7(♭9) |

He's a fool and don't I know it, But a fool can have his charms;

| Dm7 | G7 | Cmaj7 | C6 | Dm7 | G7 | Cmaj7 | C6 |

I'm in love and don't I show it, Like a babe in arms.

| Dm7 | G7 | Cmaj7 C6 | Dm7 | G7 | C | A7(♭9) |

Love's the same old sad sen - sa - tion, Late - ly I've not slept a wink,

222

I Could Write a Book

love you___ a lot, _____ Then the

world dis- - cov- ers as my book

ends, How to make two lov- ers of

friends. If they friends.___

Wait Till You See Her

Moderate waltz tempo

smoothly

My friends who knew me, Nev - er would know me,

They'd look right through me, A - bove and be - low me and

ask "who's that man? Who is that man?

Refrain *(in spirited tempo)*

Wait till you see her, see how she looks, Wait till you hear her laugh. _____ Paint-ers of paint-ings, writ-ers of books, Nev-er could tell the half. _____ Wait till you feel the warmth of her glance,

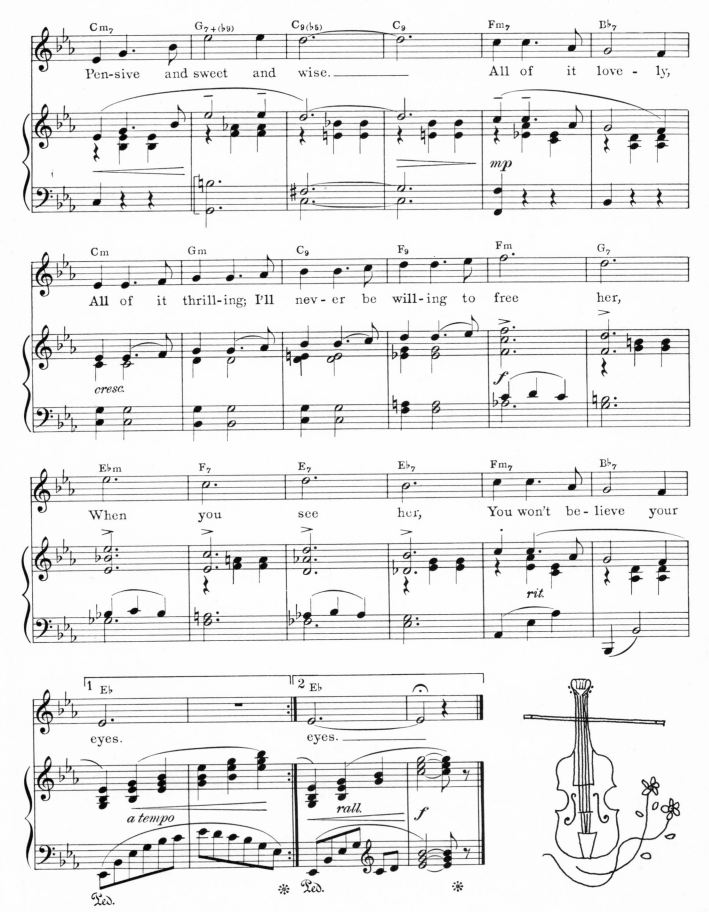

Pen-sive and sweet and wise._____ All of it love - ly,

All of it thrill-ing; I'll nev - er be will-ing to free her,

When you see her, You won't be - lieve your

eyes. eyes._____

Nobody's Heart

Leisurely

Refrain (slowly, with expression)

No-bod-y's heart be-longs to me, Heigh-ho! Who cares?

No-bod-y writes his songs to me, No___ one be-longs to me, That's the

least of my cares. I may be sad at times, And dis-in-

Go hunt - ing with pride, _____

Track bears to their lairs. _____

Ride, Am - a - zon ride! _____

Heigh-ho, ____ Who cares? _____

Dal ℅ al Fine

rit.

Index

Notes on Rodgers and Hart Shows

Appearing in This Book

GARRICK GAIETIES, I

Produced by the Theatre Guild
June 8, 1925
Garrick Theatre
Principals: Romney Brent
        June Cochrane
        Sterling Holloway
        Philip Loeb
        Edith Meiser
        Betty Starbuck
        Libby Holman
        Lee Strasberg

GARRICK GAIETIES, II

Produced by the Theatre Guild
May 10, 1926
Garrick Theatre
Principals: Romney Brent
        Sterling Holloway
        Philip Loeb
        Bobbie Perkins
        Betty Starbuck

DEAREST ENEMY

Book by Herbert Fields
Produced by George Ford
September 18, 1925
Knickerbocker Theatre
Principals: Flavia Arcaro
        Helen Ford
        Charles Purcell
        John Seymour

THE GIRL FRIEND

Book by Herbert Fields
Produced by Lew Fields
March 17, 1926
Vanderbilt Theatre
Principals: June Cochrane
        John Hundley
        Eva Puck
        Sam White

PEGGY-ANN

Book by Herbert Fields
Produced by Lew Fields and Lyle D. Andrews
December 27, 1926
Vanderbilt Theatre
Principals: Helen Ford
        Lulu McConnell
        Betty Starbuck
        Jack Thompson
        Lester Cole
        Edith Meiser

A CONNECTICUT YANKEE

Book by Herbert Fields
Produced by Lew Fields and Lyle D. Andrews
November 3, 1927
Vanderbilt Theatre
Principals: Nana Bryant
        Constance Carpenter
        William Norris
        William Gaxton
        June Cochrane

PRESENT ARMS

Book by Herbert Fields
Produced by Lew Fields
April 26, 1928
Mansfield Theatre
Principals: Joyce Barbour
        Busby Berkeley
        Charles King
        Flora Le Breton

SPRING IS HERE

Book by Owen Davis
Produced by Alex A. Aarons & Vinton Freedley
March 11, 1929
Alvin Theatre
Principals: Joyce Barbour
        Inez Courtney
        Glenn Hunter
        Charles Ruggles
        Lillian Taiz
        John Hundley

HEADS UP

Book by John McGowan and Paul Gerard Smith
Produced by Alex A. Aarons & Vinton Freedley
November 11, 1929
Alvin Theatre
Principals: Ray Bolger
      Victor Moore
      Janet Velie
      Jack Whiting
      Barbara Newberry
      Alice Boulden

SIMPLE SIMON

Book by Ed Wynn and Guy Bolton
Produced by Florenz Ziegfeld
February 18, 1930
Ziegfeld Theatre
Principals: Bobbe Arnst
      Alan Edwards
      Harriet Hoctor
      Ed Wynn
      Ruth Etting

EVERGREEN

Book by Benn Levy
Produced by Charles B. Cochran
December 3, 1930
Adelphi Theatre, London
Principals: Joyce Barbour
      Sonnie Hale
      Kay Hammond
      Jessie Matthews

AMERICA'S SWEETHEART

Book by Herbert Fields
Produced by Laurence Schwab and Frank Mandel
February 10, 1931
Broadhurst Theatre
Principals: Jeanne Aubert
      Virginia Bruce
      Harriet Lake
      John Sheehan
      Jack Whiting

JUMBO

Book by Ben Hecht and Charles MacArthur
Produced by Billy Rose
November 16, 1935
Hippodrome
Principals: Jimmy Durante
      Gloria Grafton
      A. P. Kaye
      Bob Lawrence
      Donald Novis
      Paul Whiteman and his orchestra

ON YOUR TOES

Book by Richard Rodgers, Lorenz Hart, and
   George Abbott
Produced by Dwight Deere Wiman
April 11, 1936
Imperial Theatre
Principals: Ray Bolger
      Doris Carson
      Luella Gear
      Tamara Geva
      Monty Woolley

BABES IN ARMS

Book by Lorenz Hart
Produced by Dwight Deere Wiman
April 14, 1937
Shubert Theatre
Principals: Alfred Drake
      Mitzi Green
      Ray Heatherton
      Wynn Murray
      Grace McDonald
      Ray McDonald
      Duke McHale
      Robert Rounseville

I'D RATHER BE RIGHT

Book by George S. Kaufman and Moss Hart
Produced by Sam H. Harris
November 2, 1937
Alvin Theatre
Principals: Florenz Ames
      George M. Cohan
      Joy Hodges
      Taylor Holmes
      Joseph Macaulay
      Austin Marshall
      Mary Jane Walsh

I MARRIED AN ANGEL

From Hungarian play by Janos Vaszary
Produced by Dwight Deere Wiman
May 11, 1938
Shubert Theatre
Principals: Audrey Christie
          Dennis King
          Vivienne Segal
          Walter Slezak
          Vera Zorina
          Charles Walters

THE BOYS FROM SYRACUSE

Musical comedy by George Abbott, based on
   Shakespeare's *A Comedy of Errors*
Produced by George Abbott
November 23, 1938
Alvin Theatre
Principals: Eddie Albert
          Ronald Graham
          Burl Ives
          Jimmy Savo
          Teddy Hart
          Muriel Angelus
          Marcy Wescott
          Wynn Murray

TOO MANY GIRLS

Musical comedy by George Marion, Jr.
Produced by George Abbott
October 18, 1939
Imperial Theatre
Principals: Desi Arnaz
          Eddie Bracken
          Van Johnson
          Richard Kollmar
          Hal Leroy
          Marcy Wescott
          Diosa Costello
          Mary Jane Walsh

HIGHER AND HIGHER

Musical comedy by Gladys Hurlbut and Joshua
   Logan, from idea of Irvin Pincus
Produced by Dwight Deere Wiman
April 4, 1940
Shubert Theatre
Principals: Jane Ball
          Leif Ericson
          Jack Haley
          Shirley Ross
          Marta Eggert
          Lee Dixon
          Robert Rounseville
          June Allyson

PAL JOEY

Musical comedy by John O'Hara
Produced by George Abbott
December 25, 1940
Ethel Barrymore Theatre
Principals: June Havoc
          Van Johnson
          Gene Kelly
          Vivienne Segal
          Jack Durant
          Leila Ernst

BY JUPITER

Musical comedy by Richard Rodgers &
   Lorenz Hart based on *The Warrior's Husband*
   by Julian F. Thompson
Produced by Dwight Deere Wiman and
   Richard Rodgers
June 2, 1942
Shubert Theatre
Principals: Ray Bolger
          Ronald Graham
          Constance Moore
          Benay Venuta
          Vera-Ellen
          Robert Chisholm

A CONNECTICUT YANKEE
(new production)

Book by Herbert Fields
Produced by Richard Rodgers
November 17, 1943
Martin Beck Theatre
Principals: Dick Foran
          Vivienne Segal
          Vera-Ellen
          Julie Warren

About This Book

THIS BOOK *was, of course, conceived twenty-five years ago with the beginning of the famous collaboration of Richard Rodgers and Lorenz Hart. It has come to fruition now through the collaboration of a number of other people as well, all of them convinced that the best of the Rodgers and Hart songs had to be published in one beautiful permanent volume, edited by Mr. Rodgers.*

Mr. Rodgers himself selected the forty-seven songs he felt belonged in such a book, songs which he thought best represented the team of Rodgers and Hart and which, judging by their popularity, had meant the most to song-listeners around the country. Somehow amid the pressure of work with Oscar Hammerstein II, on shows such as South Pacific *and* The King and I, *he made time to supervise art work, write an introduction, and make the final decisions which would make the book a fitting tribute to his late partner. At his request the various publishers of Rodgers and Hart sheet music agreed to lift the usual copyright restrictions on the songs, making it possible for the first time to publish all of these outstanding popular songs in one unique volume.*

Doris Lee, who besides being one of America's best-known artists, happens to be Rodgers' favorite illustrator, happily agreed to illustrate the book, and Dr. Albert Sirmay, who arranged the music in A Treasury of Gilbert and Sullivan *and has been musical editor to George Gershwin and Cole Porter as well as Richard Rodgers, made arrangements of the songs which make them easy and eminently singable for everybody.*

Oscar Hammerstein II, who is able to view the Rodgers and Hart songs from his unique vantage point as Richard Rodgers' only other collaborator, has done a preface to the book, and Richard Rodgers has written the introduction, giving intimate details of his association with Lorenz Hart. Margery Darrell, an associate editor of Simon and Schuster, has gathered together all available Rodgers and Hart anecdotes and history and added a profile of the famous collaboration.